ADVANCE PRAISE

"David Perry has compiled a ton of valuable insights into the elusive yet invaluable art of serving and delighting customers. Through anecdotes and actionable tips, Game of Sales outfits you for a successful career getting enterprise customers excited about novel solutions to their greatest problems."

—SCOTT BELSKY, FOUNDER, BEHANCE;
CHIEF PRODUCT OFFICER, ADOBE

"A valuable compilation of tips and insight for anyone in sales. David's genuine and caring approach to enterprise sales is a recipe for success."

—STEPHEN FRIEDER, PRESIDENT, ADOBE AMERICAS

"David Perry's sixty-three game changers are just that—if you want to go into enterprise sales, this is a must-read!"

—JONAH GOODHART, FORMER CEO OF MOAT (ACQUIRED BY ORACLE), ENTREPRENEUR, INVESTOR

"It simply doesn't get any better than this for enterprise sales. Tons of practical advice and lessons you can apply right now to hit your number."

—KURT BROCKWELL, ENTERPRISE SALES LEADER, AMAZON

"Resilience, adaptability, drive, and more. Games of Sales offers a range of stories and tips that all sellers can learn and apply today."

—SCOTT FALZONE, MANAGING DIRECTOR, GOOGLE

"In the sales world, there are order takers who are lucky to have hot products, and there are strategic sellers who create value by educating clients and solving their problems. David Perry's book takes you through the ins and outs of what it means to think and operate like a strategic seller."

—PAUL BRODY, FORMER VICE PRESIDENT, IBM

"Finally, a book that shows how hardball tactics and one-upmanship are ancient relics of the past. Game of Sales powerfully argues that caring about client needs and capturing hidden value are the key aspects of effective dealmaking."

—JACK HERSEY, FORMER GENERAL MANAGER
AND VICE PRESIDENT, MICROSOFT

"While sharing his experience working for the industry giants— Adobe, Amazon, Google, and IBM—David tells you how to think big with your offer, uncover hidden value, and find a straighter path to success."

—ALEX CHEN, FORMER GLOBAL ACCOUNT
DIRECTOR, LINKEDIN; FORMER STRATEGIC
ACCOUNT EXECUTIVE, APPLE

"An enterprise sales book for the ages. Get a sneak peek into the life of an enterprise salesperson, learn how some of the largest, most successful technology companies in the world operate, and find a roadmap to success whether you are just starting your career in technology sales or are a seasoned professional. Read this book now!"

—RICK VALENZUELA, STRATEGIC ACCOUNT DIRECTOR, TWILIO; FORMERLY STRATEGIC ACCOUNT DIRECTOR AT TABLEAU AND AKAMAI

"Amazing advice for enterprise salespeople and those starting out to consistently meet and exceed your sales goals."

—BRIAN COHEN, CHAIRMAN, NEW YORK ANGELS

"Fun, engaging stories, plus proven sales strategies? Yes, please! What's not to love? Every enterprise salesperson and startup CEO should read this book."

—COOPER HARRIS, CEO, KLICKLY

"With a refreshing touch of humor and depth of real-world knowledge, Game of Sales is full of personal stories that coach as well as entertain. This book is a must-have in your sales arsenal!"

—MARK CROFTON, GLOBAL VICE PRESIDENT, SAP

GAME OF SALES

GAME OF SALES

LESSONS LEARNED WORKING AT ADOBE, AMAZON, GOOGLE, AND IBM

DAVID PERRY

LIONCREST
PUBLISHING

GAME OF SALES
Lessons Learned Working at Adobe, Amazon, Google, and IBM

ISBN   978-1-5445-0221-2 *Paperback*
       978-1-5445-0220-5 *Ebook*

This book is dedicated to my wife Arianne whose love, support, and drive inspires me every day.

CONTENTS

ACKNOWLEDGMENTS

A sincere thank you to the following people who have contributed in their own wonderfully unique ways to make this book possible:

Aaron Bell, Aaron Hill, Adil Allamar, AJ Jordan, Alan Nathan, Albert Ko, Alex Chen, Alex Fishbeyn, Alex Rogers, Alex Walter, Alexis I. Candee, Alia Singh, Alicia Perry, Alison Reichert, Allen Jeffries, Andrew Hirshman, Andrew Weinreich, Andy Friedland, Anil Chakravarthy, Anil Hinduja, Ann Lewnes, Anthony Colarullo, Anthony Malangone, Antonio Sciuto, Aparna Menon, Arianne Perry, Artur Krillov, Athena Perry, Barbara Minto, Ben Djavieri, Benjy Federbush, Bill Sellers, Blake Marin, Brad Rencher, Brad Snyder, Brannen McDonald, Brian Cohen, Brian Wirth, Carl Brungaber, Cary Goss, Chip Scovic, Chris Elser, Chris Fong, Chris Helin, Chris Longden, Chris Ohlhoff, Chris Young, Cindy Curtis, Cliff Lerner, Cooper Harris, Dan Tyre, Dan Wellers, Daniel Hsu, David Caissie, Dave Andersen, David Fontanez, David Liu, Dennis Apo, Dianne Anderson, Diego Leal Ambriz, Doni Lillis, Donna Morris, Ed Lopez, Ehren Hozumi, Emily Anderson, Emily deRegrt, Emily Griffith, Eric Kroll, Fernando Bazan,

Gary Caunitis, Geoff Ramsey, Greg Galant, Griffin Camper, Henry Perry, Imran Afab, Jack Hersey, James Stewart, James Timberlake, Jamie LeFrak, Jason van Namen, Jay Nielson, Jean English, Jeff Figueredo, Jela Bubic, Jeremy Hurst, Jeremy Pincus, Jim Lecinski, Jocelyn de Almeida, John Lecrone, John Sharpe, Jonah Goodhart, Julie Rollauer, Juliette Vick, Justin Merickel, Kamau Brown, Karl Saxe, Keith Eadie, Kelly Eng, Ken Hoffman, Kevin Howard, Kurt Brockwell, Kris Edwards, Kyle Keogh, Lana Silva, Laura Mazzarino, Leslie Myers, Lisa Nielsen, Lisa Utzschneider, Marc Perry, Marco Turner, Mary Perry, Matt Downing, Matt Thompson, Michael Greenberg, Michael Lacy, Michael Librizzi, Mike Lacerenza, Mitch Nelson, Myrna Newman, Nancy Pearson, Nate Winn, Nick Gross, Nicole Boritz, Neil Coleman, Paul Brody, Peter Brine, Rick McAninch, Rob Rosenthal, Rob Williams, Robbie Traube, Robert Painter, Robert Walsh, Robyn Myers, Russel Wirth, Ryan Mayward, Sal Scilingo, Sandie Hawkins, Sarah Falck, Saurabh Singh, Scott Belsky, Scott Gifis, Sean Cross, Serge Kassardjian, Shane Herrell, Shantanu Narayen, Shauzab Ladha, Stephen Frieder, Steve Sackler, Steven Fay, Steve Gomez, Steven Plous, Suraj Chauhan, Susan Sheffield, Terence Woolf, Thomas Reese, Tim Braz, Tim Hackenberg, Tim Murdoch, Todd Underwood, Tommy Oudinot, Tucker Max, Varun Bhansali, Warren Gardner, Wojciech Dojka, Yilian Pei, Yuni Sameshima, Zach Johnson, Zach Obront, and Zephan Fischl.

To access additional Game of Sales materials,
visit https://www.gameofsalesbook.com.

INTRODUCTION

"If you really look closely, most overnight successes took a long time."

—STEVE JOBS, AMERICAN BUSINESS ICON

Imagine sitting in a conference room with over 2,000 enterprise salespeople watching a video that highlights the awesome sales year you had. Somehow, that's where I found myself during the 2018 annual sales kickoff for Adobe in Las Vegas.

The film was a tongue-in-cheek production about how Adobe rocks, along with a little over-the-top recognition of my sales performance during the previous twelve months. It begins with me sitting in a plush tan Swedish lounge chair with a magnificent mountain vista view in the background. As the camera pans out, it reveals the office I was casually enjoying belongs to Adobe's EVP & GM, and I'm drinking from the man's personalized coffee mug.

Unless you've worked at Adobe, you probably don't know who our EVP & GM at the time was, but his lofty stature atop the organizational hierarchy, and constant on-stage presence at our company events gave him larger-than-life status. And there I am for the entire company to see (including the man himself) in a larger-than-life, high-definition video production, as if we were best friends and had some sort of *mi casa es su casa* arrangement.

It's a ridiculous narrative, but the script had executives and colleagues texting me for months afterward, saying how funny they thought it was and how much they loved it. Most of them said something like, "Dave, I had no idea you were funny!" I'm unsure if that was a compliment or not, but I took it as a positive regardless. Even better, our GM approached me a few months later and told me, "Great job with the video!"

I'm not sure if he meant great job with the comic performance, great job closing deals, or both. Regardless of his motivation for the atta-boy, that moment was instant career validation for me. I was officially recognized and appreciated by someone so influential in the technology space, that his decisions shaped the way our industry functions.

That short won the distinction of being named the *Best Prod-*

uct Commercial among several other competitors (many of which had some serious production value going for them) in the film festival portion of the festivities. I remember thinking to myself, "What the hell did I do to deserve all this attention? How did I get here?"

I always prided myself on going the extra mile, being a team player, and doing what's best for my company and our clients, but I never considered myself special, certainly not to the point of warranting any sort of celebrity-style recognition. What created such a moment of surrealistic achievement for me that day?

The best explanation was that I had an outstanding year. In fact, I had closed the largest deal on my team of thirty for three of the previous five quarters. In case you're not familiar with enterprise sales, closing the largest deal on your team even once can be a career-defining moment. Doing it twice puts you in elite company. Accomplishing such a feat three quarters out of five is absurd, almost to the point of being unbelievable.

Full disclosure: I didn't execute any of these deals alone. They all required the serious dedication, collaboration, and expertise of a full team of highly skilled colleagues.

If you're asking, "Okay, I get it; you had a great sales year at Adobe, Dave. Congratulations, but why should I care? Why do I need to know about it? And why should I read the rest of your book?"

You should care because I didn't do anything that any other enterprise salesperson with a strong work ethic and a desire to elevate can't do. My point is that I can tell you exactly how I got here, so you can apply the same principles to your career.

That culmination of success for me didn't magically happen overnight; I made no deals with the devil; and I certainly didn't do anything immoral or unethical. The truth is, to level-up your professional life and achieve success in sales, you don't need to do any of those things.

Most important, I wrote this book because I wish I had something like it when I went through the moments in my career that weren't so great—the times that were filled with anxiety, doubt, and fear.

Knowing then what I know now would have made my career path much straighter and smoother.

There's nothing I can do about the past, but there is something I can do about the future. If this book helps you in any way to avoid some of the challenges I experienced but still enjoy the incredible rewards our industry has to offer, this writing will have been a tremendously successful endeavor for both of us.

Hopefully, you'll find this book to be a refreshing, enjoyable, and purposeful difference-maker in your career. Throughout these pages, we'll explore some vital sales lessons that I learned the hard way that can help everybody from the enterprise sales newbie to the veteran looking for an edge.

For instance, I'll talk about how a mindset based on caring and a genuine desire to have the best interest of all stakeholders in a deal is far more efficient than any hardball negotiating tactics. By staying true to this concept of caring, you'll learn about the art of finding hidden value, which can level-up your deal-making.

You'll also learn about some proven systems and frameworks I've developed that should help you to maintain a consistent pipeline of deals.

Throughout the book, I'll dedicate time to hard lessons learned through temporary setbacks like horrible meetings and tough conversations; both are experiences every enterprise salesperson must confront at some point in their careers.

Later in the book, you'll read about some effective ways I've learned to organize deal teams and get them firing on all cylinders.

Finally, the last chapter will discuss the art of searching for, working, and closing potentially career-defining mega deals. Sure, this is the money maker, but please resist skipping to this section. It really won't help much without the other chapters.

A career in enterprise sales is one of the most exciting, interesting, and potentially lucrative ways to make a living. While the road to success isn't always lined with champagne and rose petals, the rewards of mastering the craft can be glorious. That's what this book is all about.

To begin, chapter 1 will provide a detailed exploration of my perspective on why enterprise sales is awesome. That's an important concept, because I want to make sure you feel that way too. I hope you learn something from these pages and enjoy the experience. Let the journey begin!

PART 1

INSPIRATION AND PERSPECTIVE

CHAPTER 1

WHY ENTERPRISE SALES IS AWESOME!

"Choose a job you love, and you will never have to work a day in your life."

—CONFUCIUS (ANCIENT PHILOSOPHER, TEACHER, AND POLITICIAN)

Our society offers a nearly infinite number of choices to earn a respectable living. You could be an accountant, web designer, greeting card writer, stunt double, etc. I would argue that none of those professions, however, offer the same potential for reward, freedom, and excitement as a career in sales. Okay, maybe being a stunt double is more exciting than sales, but there's significantly more risk involved with that as a career choice.

My route to sales was not a straight line. Fortunately, my background in other key functional areas such as business analysis and consulting showed me just how great a career in sales could really be.

Although I've always gravitated toward the revenue generating side of business, I began my career as an analyst and consultant. During that phase of my professional life, I recall a pivotal moment that steered me toward the path of sales.

At the time, I was working with a business analyst and programmer who was absolutely brilliant. He learned our company's proprietary development language inside and out to create an extremely useful and unique piece of mapping software. The program enabled our company to translate data sources seamlessly, to create consolidated financial reporting for ultra-high-net-worth individuals and top institutions. The achievement was nothing short of amazing, and it became the foundation for a $100 million revenue stream for the company.

From an individual career perspective, I thought there was a big problem with that situation—lack of portability. That guy's talent was undeniable and his contribution to the company's bottom line was stupendous. But once he built that software, he was expendable, as his work was finished. From that point forward, programmers with much lesser skillsets could maintain everything, and he couldn't take any of his hard work with him because everything he built was in an obscure internal-only programming language, tied to esoteric systems with highly specialized use. That caused me to reflect on my own situation.

As a business analyst, I was in a similar position. I couldn't take my skillset with me to another company, and if I created a similar $100 million revenue stream, I wouldn't get to participate in the upside.

That particular organization was also in the midst of being

acquired, so we were going through several rounds of layoffs, which made me realize that the idea of job security was beginning to vanish; a suspicion that, since then, has fully evolved into a stark reality of today's economy.

At that moment, however, I decided that I didn't want to be subject to the volatility of a potentially unstable profession any longer, and I made the commitment to choose a much more portable career path; one where I could develop a skill set that wouldn't lose all value when I left a particular role.

ULTIMATE MARKETABILITY

I wanted to work in an industry where my skills would be more marketable from one company to the next. If the days of a twenty-year career with a singular organization were over— as popular opinion told us, even back in the early 2000s—it only makes sense to have a career that would allow you to flow seamlessly between opportunities, while building upon previous successes. That was the biggest factor in my decision to embark on a sales career in the first place. I soon realized that companies of all types and sizes in all industries are on the sales table. It's a profession that provides ultimate marketability.

Sales allows people to move from one opportunity to the next without any crippling fear of extended joblessness. In a worst-case scenario, you could find yourself in a company that isn't a good fit—for whatever reason—and you need to leave. As long as you're committed to success, you'll soon land another role. In fact, if you've demonstrated an aptitude for selling, you'll have multiple offers from other companies lined up, perhaps before you depart.

The bottom line is, if you are committed to your craft, and have the desire to create revenue for a company, sales will allow you to write your own ticket.

LARGE VERSUS SMALL COMPANIES: THE CHOICE IS YOURS

Sales can take you anywhere you want to go. You can live in the high-visibility, fast-paced world of enterprise sales and close megadeals for the most impactful companies of our time, like Adobe, Amazon, Google, and IBM. Or you could sell for a much smaller company where your performance will have a much larger impact on the overall success of the organization. If neither of those options ramp up your meter for career excitement enough, perhaps you'll become the Chief Revenue Officer of a start-up or even create your own company, where you can build something from nothing and watch it grow.

Understand that smaller companies may not have the budget to send the entire workforce to Las Vegas for an all-expenses-paid, weekend-long festival of fun. However, you most likely will have the opportunity to partner with bigger companies and attend their sales kick-offs and customer conferences, as well as other high-profile industry events.

If you work in sales, at a large or small company, the sky is the limit, but know that what happens in Vegas doesn't necessarily stay in Vegas when you're there with 2,000 coworkers.

Take a look at the table below for a typical listing of the differing benefits from working at large or small companies. Then, decide which one suits you best. Also, don't be afraid to try a small company for now and a large one later, or vice-versa.

You might have to experience both options before you know which one you prefer.

THE BENEFITS OF A CAREER IN SALES AT LARGE VS. SMALL COMPANIES

LARGE COMPANY	SMALL COMPANY
• Market access via brand recognition	• Access via innovative niche offerings
• World-class executive leadership	
• Multitudes of systems and processes to learn and leverage	• Unstructured environment
	• Opportunity to develop business process and select systems to support your functional role
• High-caliber onboarding and ongoing training	
• Stable compensation plans with less downside but with capped upside	• Equity with life-changing exit potential
	• Potential for uncapped compensation and/or higher percentage of deals
• Restricted stock units (with immediate value)	
• Stable territory alignment annually, sometimes year-over-year	• Variable territory and compensation plans
• Focus on one industry, subsegment, or client	• Increased likelihood to be involved in hiring decisions
• Internal mobility	• Increased potential for upward mobility

Game Changer #1: Enterprise sales is an elite profession with significant lateral and upward mobility. Outside of executive leadership, the highest earners at most companies, large and small, are the top salespeople.

IT'S A WONDERFUL LIFE

A career in sales means much more than having a highly marketable skillset. It also means that you're going to have access to some of the most incredible experiences the world has to offer, especially if you choose to work in enterprise technology sales. How many other professions offer these benefits?

- If you like to travel, a career in sales is a no-brainer. Conferences and vacations are just one form of the travel involved. You could—and likely will—travel all over the country and even the world—depending on your role—to visit clients, partners, and other key players involved in various deals.
- Sales allows you to build a powerful and expansive network, consisting of some of the most influential and high-profile executives in the world. Better yet, the value of that network grows over time, as your peers and clients break off into different companies.
- Opportunities to refine and master your craft will be present throughout your career. As such, deals will become easier to close and bigger deals become more doable. Eventually, mega-deals begin to surface and from there, anything is possible!
- Unlike a career in law or consulting, you're not trading time for money in sales. The two assets are not directly exchangeable. Instead, the more skilled you become at your craft, the less time it takes to close deals. Soon enough, you'll learn how to make more money in less time than you ever thought possible. A meeting over coffee or a chance encounter at a conference could lead to a transformational deal and change your prospects overnight.
- The skills you build will retain value as you move from one company to another. There is no such thing as job security anymore, but sales is extremely portable and allows you to make yourself indispensably valuable. Marketability is rarely a concern in this profession.

- A career in sales can provide access to perks that you're unlikely to receive in other professions. Among other things, sales can give you access to private shows, conferences in Vegas with non-stop parties and events, and lavish vacation getaways to exotic locales.

I've been fortunate enough in my career to experience all of those things, and you can too.

GOOGLE (AT) PLAY

In 2010, I landed at Google. Getting a job at a company as big and impactful as that was a huge win for me. While I had been fortunate to work at IBM, which was an enormous company with tremendous industry influence, that was an organization steeped in tradition with proven systems and processes on a global scale. That business dynamic is certainly an outstanding thing to be a part of, but I was excited about the change of pace that Google was going to offer. Their focus on consumer-facing applications, in particular, was something new and exciting for me.

Google increasingly redefines how we think about the future and continues to have an enormous impact on the internet. Even back then, their products were used by hundreds of millions of people all over the world. So, yes, I was more than a little excited to have a chance to work for them.

Big tech is famous for rewarding employees with some unbelievable perks, and there's a good reason for that reputation. For instance, my career at Google began with a surreal moment. Their NYC headquarters occupies an entire city block on 8th Avenue between 15th and 16th Streets. During one of my first days at work, I walked in and heard music coming from the main meeting area on the fourth floor...

It sounded like the song *Sweet Disposition* by the band, The Temper Trap, which happened to be one of my favorite songs at the time. Sure enough, when I opened the door, I was right. Temper Trap was recording a video to post on YouTube. About twenty of us who happened to stop by the studio in NYC that day got to enjoy their performance for free!

Some companies treat meeting attendees to coffee and pastries; Google gives them rock bands.

I don't know what the going rate is to have a rock band play a private show, but it seems like an event some people would pay several thousand dollars for. Yet, I got the experience for free because of where I was employed.

Google doesn't hold a sales conference every year, but when they do, it's first-class all the way. One year, they hosted one that was absolutely epic! On that occasion, they took over the Palazzo at the Venetian in Las Vegas. The entire building—from top-to-bottom—was wall-to-wall Google.

That sales conference wasn't exclusively about the accommodations. The company also hosted one party after another, and scheduled incredible events with live music, top performers, and more, where all the concessions were free. They even rented out the arena for the UNLV basketball team to host a Bruno Mars concert. Once again, they didn't merely rent out a few rows or even an entire section. Google rented out the entire arena, which was capable of holding over 19,000 people.

There was plenty of corporate education happening as well. Google smartly seized the opportunity to enlighten its employees in the midst of such revelry, by hosting several conference sessions that informed everyone about the exciting plans for the future of the company. Work hard, play hard!

They're not the only company that goes big with their sales conferences. Google might go a little over-the-top on occasion, but Adobe does the same thing and throws in reward trips as well. Just about every big-tech organization I've worked for, or with, treats their sales staff the same way. It really is a wonderful life!

ALOHA ADOBE

In addition to worldwide sales kickoffs and several major customer conferences, each year Adobe takes all its top-performing salespeople and executives to an amazing location for a week of pampering. They even invite significant others to participate in the indulgence. For example, when I had my blowout year, my wife and I were invited to join other top performers and executives for a getaway to Maui as a reward.

As soon as we touched down on the island, they handed each of us pairs of Maui Jim sunglasses and spending money. They also reserved beautiful rooms, treated us to gourmet dinners and provided access to numerous Hawaiian-style adventures like all-terrain vehicle tours, ocean rafting, and surfing lessons. In fact, they presented my wife and I with a different gift item every day. The whole trip was such an incredible experience, it caused my wife to look at me and say, "Okay, you need to get us back here every year!"

The defining moment of that Hawaiian getaway for me

occurred while surfing with my wife. It was one of the most breathtaking experiences either of us has ever had. I remember cruising by a gathering of sea turtles, while riding the waves underneath a clear blue sky, complete with rainbows showering us with a spectrum of colors in the distance. It was a scene I couldn't have pictured taking place anywhere else in the world, certainly not where I live, in NYC. I also couldn't have pictured that moment being possible if I was working any other corporate job. Shortly after we took in the views of the colorful sky and ocean creatures, I rode the longest wave of my life and one of my instructors high-fived me on my way by.

These are just a small sample of reasons why sales is awesome. Sales has also given me the chance to lead elite teams and partner with some of the world's most influential executives to create deals that alter the way huge companies operate. It's an incredible feeling to be a part of a dynamic where you feel the support and excitement of having the entire company behind you to get the deal done.

Game Changer #2: Closing a deal is one of the most exciting experiences in business. Each time you make it happen, you'll learn how to do it bigger, better, and faster.

ACCESS TO MOVERS AND SHAKERS

I once witnessed a conversation between Eric Schmidt, who was the executive chairman of Google, talking to Sal Khan, who is the founder of Khan Academy and one of the greatest innovators in education of our time. These are people who shape our lives with their innovation and creativity.

As part of the sales process, I've been able to participate in such conversations with similarly high-profile executives from many companies.

In one particularly memorable meeting, I met with Jeff Blackburn (otherwise known as Jeff Bezos's second in command), Lisa Utzschneider, former lead of Amazon Media Group, and the senior leadership team from a multi-billion-dollar division of Nestle, which included their top marketer, sales leader, and strategist.

We discussed a plan I put forth to build a strategic partnership that would deliver enormous value to Nestle and increase Amazon's revenue stream for our advertising business from a few hundred thousand dollars to several million dollars in one year. Today, that would be a somewhat insignificant deal for them, but back then, it was actually a big number.

My point is that bringing people with that kind of firepower together can shape the results for big companies for an entire year or more. During that meeting, we revolutionized that division's approach to ecommerce. It's an incredible feeling to be part of something like that.

Another brush with greatness occurred when I was called on stage for making Club as a top performer, and Shantanu Narayen, Adobe's CEO, shook my hand and called me by name. Shantanu is the type of CEO that comes along once in a generation. I was thrilled to meet him, and I can't imagine that would have happened had I done anything else with my career.

Game Changer #3: Sales will allow you to meet and even work with the top business leaders in the world.

The point of these reminiscences isn't to be braggadocios in any way about my own career. Many of the salespeople I've worked with, who have stuck with it, have similar or better stories to tell. There are many paths to success. If you traverse the road to enterprise sales as your career destination, I guarantee you'll also get to work with some of the greatest minds in the world.

WHAT MAKES FOR A GREAT ENTERPRISE SALESPERSON?

There's a popular misconception about sales that prevents a lot of people from exploring a career in it. I'm talking about an unfair stigma that paints a portrait of the typical salesperson as a pushy, dishonest fast-talker. Contrary to this decades-old stereotype, the great enterprise salespeople I've worked with have been forthright, hard-working, and caring individuals, who have tremendous drive and can come from all walks of life.

It really doesn't matter if you're an extrovert, introvert, or ambivert—you can become great at sales with your own style. When I think about all the top salespeople I've met, there are commonalities, but their overall approaches, talent, and salient qualities can differ radically. As such, I'm convinced that anyone can be successful in enterprise sales, as long as they're focused and have the drive to do it.

> Game Changer #4: Top enterprise salespeople are teammates, consultants, analysts, product experts, project managers, and leaders. How do you stack up in these areas?

At this point, hopefully you're excited to move forward with a new sales career. One where you can achieve satisfaction, excitement, and rewards that just aren't possible in most other roles.

Soon, you'll learn about proven systems and frameworks to help you win at the game of sales. Later on, you'll learn about some nuances I've discovered that can help you to fine-tune your craft. Eventually, I'll talk about mega deals, how to create them, and what they can mean for your career.

The next chapter, however, will show you how to learn from the best by researching crucial technology trends and industry leaders. More specifically, it will demonstrate the importance of acquiring expansive industry knowledge to seamlessly transform client conversations into opportunities and win over senior executives.

CHAPTER 2

RAMP-UP ON INDUSTRY LEADERS AND TECHNOLOGY

"These days you better become a subject matter expert, in addition to a salesperson."
—BRANNEN MCDONALD (DIRECTOR GLOBAL
STRATEGY & EXECUTION, ADOBE)

Getting a handle on the industry landscape is one of the most important things you can do to take your sales career to the next level. By ramping up your knowledge in whatever industry you work in (oil and gas, retail, healthcare, technology, or anything else), as well as the leaders who control those organizations, you'll build instant credibility to secure meetings, win over senior executives, and seamlessly convert conversations into opportunities without *pitching*.

Technology is another key aspect of your knowledge arsenal. It's eating the world, as we know it. Everything from watches and refrigerators to light bulbs and televisions is smart and on-demand. Therefore, it doesn't matter if you work for Google or Walmart, you must know as much as possible about trending technology.

Sales is no different from anything else when it comes to technology. The profession is evolving in parallel with technology and it's doing so at a rapid pace; one where many individuals may struggle to keep up. Don't let that be you. Stay aware of the data-driven changes taking place in sales and be able to converse about technology with anyone at any time.

By the end of this chapter, you'll have a much deeper understanding of how to think about enterprise technology companies. This will provide you with an excellent foundation for ramping up your industry knowledge, and the way technology is shaping our world.

As examples, I'm going to share insight into what it's like working at Adobe, Amazon, Google, and IBM. This should give you a good start to apply specific industry knowledge to client conversations and catch the attention of senior executives. Then, you can build on that foundation with your own additional research.

 Game Changer #5: Track the leaders of your chosen industry or vertical. Notice what's unique about their product lines, go-to market approaches, and their internal as well as external investments. If publicly traded, review 10-K sections one and seven for business overview and key financial performance metrics respectively.

ILLUMINATING IBM

In 2005, I landed at IBM, my first large enterprise technology role. On my first day, I drove up to the office complex in Somers, NY. I arrived at a security gate with a long winding driveway behind it. The campus was nowhere in sight. It was a forest-lined road, and a deer or two darted across as I was driving. Traveling up to the entryway felt like I was arriving at a billionaire's home for some sort of exclusive event.

Designed by the world-famous architect I.M. Pei, the Somers campus consisted of four buildings adorned in reflective glass that were set around a pyramid as the central structure. This created a sense of expansiveness within the complex that extended to a mindset well beyond the walls. In true IBM style, a single layout was used for each building around the pyramid as if one side of the campus was a mirror image of the other. The replicated blueprint allowed for beautiful symmetry and cost savings.

By acquiring inside knowledge of IBM, I became privy to how a company of such behemoth proportions operates. I developed a genuine feeling for what it's like to be part of an organization that has hundreds of separate marketing budgets within the Americas alone and over 350,000 employees.

IBM provided me with an incredible education into one of the most complex and matrixed organizations in the world. I saw, firsthand, how a consulting and systems integration company could implement a *tip of the arrow* approach to the addressable market and increase opportunity size.

One of the ways this works is a consulting team identifies a major opportunity and passes it along to the most appropriate, capable sales team or business unit within the organization. That team then assembles the ideal bundle of products and services (referred to as *the solution*) to meet the specific needs of the client early in the sales process. The solution is then supported by a full assessment, business case, and implementation plan. The *tip of the arrow* in such a scenario refers to the strategy consulting team that kicked off the process. They engage the client at senior levels to provide an entry point for the company to form a partnership with them.

For our purposes, the *tip of the arrow* approach enables salespeople to uncover or create big initial opportunities that could be broken up and handed down to various teams. For example, ten to fifteen years ago, middleware was used extensively to manage transactions, databases, device communication, etc. If business problems could be solved with enhancements to that layer of infrastructure, IBM could begin with that simple fix and use a strategy consulting engagement to scale the opportunity, ultimately mapping out a comprehensive solution to meet the more holistic business objectives of the organization.

That solution would involve a combination of services and technology, where various teams with different specializations would consult in various areas such as organizational change, operational strategy, software development, and others. With such a strategy, I was equipped to initiate the deployment of massive teams handling massive engagements. That same basic approach has been adopted by many of the top enterprise technology companies. Although there has been a major shift recently to cloud-based operations, the approach is still used in the current marketplace.

My IBM experience showed me how there are always multiple decision makers within large organizations that you need to win over to get a deal done. I learned quickly how to manage a variety of stakeholders, map out processes, and sell complex concepts both internally and to clients.

Game Changer #6: By ramping up your knowledge of IBM, particularly from an organizational structure standpoint, even the most complex clients will seem easy to navigate.

What proved to be a challenge while working there was that everything became very IBM-centric. The company is so big that it almost serves as its own country. It was like working in a bubble where everything outside felt less important. People can get trapped into thinking only in terms of IBM, and it became difficult to take into account emerging trends that IBM wasn't directly driving. But people who can align IBM initiatives and/or solutions effectively with those of IBM's clients in the outside world, have a chance to create major value.

I had the advantage of acquiring first-hand knowledge of IBM's organizational structure by working there. You, however, could have a different advantage in your favor. You'll have the open mind of someone evaluating a company's needs from the outside, with the critical knowledge of how the most complex companies run their business as well.

Game Changer #7: Seek to understand how industry leaders organize their businesses, and how specific functions either do or do not run across geographies, business units, or product lines and why.

UNDERSTANDING THE STRUCTURE OF COMPLEX ORGANIZATIONS

What makes IBM such a complex organization is that it can be described in terms of product and divisional structures, regions, matrixed teams, teams assembled around initiatives, and more.

SMALL COMPANY, BIG MEETINGS

In 2008, the market was burning down in a sub-prime mortgage apocalypse. The country was on the brink of a full-scale economic collapse. It was a time period where it seemed like one out of every two friends you had were getting laid off and new job prospects were few and far between.

After a year-and-a-half or so of successful business development in the U.S. and considering the instability of the economic environment, my team at IBM decided it was moving to Prague. Unfortunately, even an industry giant like IBM wasn't immune to the ills that were plaguing the U.S. economy of the time. The company was also experiencing significant layoffs, and internal hiring was frozen, which meant if I didn't relocate, I most likely would have been laid off.

Of course, I could have gone to the Czech Republic with my team, but leaving the states at that point in my life wasn't nearly as appealing as it was for others on my team. I had too much going for me here. All this turmoil placed me in a bit of career quandary at the time.

I remember sitting in IBM's office, overlooking Madison Square while on the phone with IBM's relocation team in an effort to keep my options open. I hung up the phone a bit discouraged at the unappealing nature of the options that were put before me, so the next call I made was to my brother, who had founded a fitness-focused company.

He agreed to meet me for coffee the next day and help me brainstorm solutions for my next career move. Finally, I told him that I really didn't want to relocate overseas, and he told me that if I decided to start my own business, he would help me set up the LLC and everything else I needed to get started. That was enough to convince me to start my own B2B business development consultancy called RevSpring.

The purpose of RevSpring, which I put on stasis when I joined Google, was to help startups gain access to large enterprises in exchange for cash and equity. While I was starting the business, I attended a different entrepreneurship or technology-related event almost every other weeknight. I also used LinkedIn to reach out to CEOs of the most exciting startups I could find. That became a surprisingly effective way for me to acquire clients.

RevSpring's main goal was to help its clients break into large companies. We did that by connecting them with other members of my existing and developing network, as well as generating leads through my business development lead, who was my only full-time employee. Another area of focus was to help clients create pitches and prepare all the necessary information to get in front of those bigger organizations.

As a result of this routine area of focus, I realized I developed the ability to walk into larger companies strictly as Dave Perry, without IBM or another corporate giant backing me.

A few weeks later, I was back in the same coffee shop where I met my brother. This time, however, I was meeting with an executive, ironing out the details of the demo we needed to run for his business. We also had to work out the specifics of a series of documents that were required to get in front of his Chief Security Officer.

Why was I able to get face time with these huge companies in a business environment that made it difficult for my clients and others to get the same meeting?

I realized the answer was that I built instant credibility with top executives from those companies, because I learned to ramp up very quickly on the industry landscape in which they operated. My background with IBM gave me an expansive view of the technology landscape back then, and my consulting background forced me to become an industry expert in a highly condensed timeframe. I mention this because I'm going to tell you how to do the same.

At the time, every company began to realize that technology was becoming the business, so understanding it was getting increasingly important. That aspect of the sales landscape hasn't changed and probably never will. If anything, everything has become more tech-centric today. Technology continues to accelerate at an exponential pace.

Conversing with clients about how technology was changing their industry gave me a natural segue to introduce the software or platform I was selling. This allowed me to empathize with my client and address the specific problems they were experiencing.

Every startup views the world and their industry through a unique lens. If you can speak your client's language, understand their point of view, and apply your industry knowledge according to those commonalities, you can build a specific value proposition for them or—in the very least—paint a picture of how things can work.

Game Changer #8: Match industry knowledge with the specific value proposition of your company to win credibility and open opportunities with senior executives.

GOOGLING GOOGLE

In October of 2010, I rejoined the enterprise technology world when I landed a position within the Large Client Sales organization at Google. No conversation involving the best of the best in technology is complete without mentioning this company, because Google is, was, and likely always will be full of some of the world's greatest innovators, futurists, and game-changers. Needless to say, this was an amazing opportunity for me.

Among an expanding list of high-tech superlatives, Google is also astoundingly transparent, which is the thing I admired most about working there.

In my first few weeks of working for Google, I went to a town hall meeting where Eric Schmidt, CEO at the time, delivered a surprisingly dense and highly detailed talk concerning Google's performance and plans by product line and business unit. I had seen him deliver compelling external talks before, but I was amazed at the intense level of detail and data he communicated in his internal briefings.

It was enthralling to see the leader of an industry giant talk so openly about the direction of his business, and foster the culture of transparency even further by answering a myriad of hard hitting completely unfiltered employee questions afterward. He was calm and direct. It was a refreshing and entertaining conversation with everyday employees on his team. I had never seen anything like it.

Such a meeting made me feel beyond excited because I felt like more than an individual contributor. I felt like I was part of a machine that was going to shape the future of work, the internet, advertising, and so much more through technology, and in reality, I was.

Google's level of transparency went far beyond the words of the executive chairperson. A quick search of their intranet revealed similar information detailing the long-range plans of specific technology like Google Play, Android, Google Docs, and others. Keep in mind; this took place years before many of those products became part of the technological mainstream.

One of the more ambitious and ridiculously named projects I researched was called Project Loon, when Google was trying to map the entire world with internet access via balloons that would self-modulate their position relative to each other with artificial intelligence. The balloons were to float into the upper atmosphere and cover enough area to blanket the world. I'm not kidding! In comparison, Google Glass seemed like a small idea.

Project Loon is a good example of what you'll find if you take even five minutes to look at Google X, which is the web home for Google's moonshot projects. I definitely recommend checking that out. If nothing else, it's an entertaining read.

The good news is, you don't need to be inside the organization to gain a tremendous amount of information about what Google is currently doing and where it's headed. There is a nearly endless volume of insight documented all over the internet about the company's plans and ventures.

Take some time to google...Google, and research some projects in which they're investing. Find out: How are they using their tools? What's changing with their advertising business? What are some issues they're facing?

By researching Google, you'll get more than just a glimpse of the future. You'll see what updates are coming for artificial intelligence, robotics, life extension, global internet deployment, etc. You'll see how it will affect careers, businesses, and industries. You'll see how Google is responding to changing market conditions. All this information can lead to very compelling conversations with clients and position you for successful interactions that can lead to sales.

Game Changer #9: Visit Google's website for an incredible amount of information concerning all of their products. Google's moonshot projects are spawning fledgling industries of their own and can be fascinating conversation starters.

Recommended Resource: *The Singularity Is Near* by Ray Kurzweil. Although some may consider this book to be a "little far out there," there's no denying this book can help anyone to drive intense conversations about the role technology will play in our future. The book covers the evolution of computing, human-machine interfaces, major trends in nanotechnology, robotics, and many more interesting talking points.

I was already a fan of Ray Kurzweil when I worked at Google. I read *The Singularity is Near* and immediately came to the conclusion that Kurzweil was one of the most important thinkers of our time, given the fact that he identified the law of exponential returns as a natural law of progress by tracing the history of information technology back to a census report from the 1890s.

Kurzweil pointed out that technology has undergone steady exponential progress from that time, and it has continued despite recession, depression, and war. From punch cards to vacuum tubes, transistors, integrated circuits, and soon quantum circuits, information technology has shown a steady exponential progression. Kurzweil supported his hypothesis by stating, "The phone you hold in your pocket is a billion times more powerful than the computer I worked on in the sixties that took up most of a building."

In addition, he's tracked about one hundred different indices of information technology over the past forty or so years and was able to predict when a computer would beat the world's best at Jeopardy and other games requiring advanced intelligence, among many other predictions he made decades in advance.

One day someone on my Google team said, "Dave, guess who we just hired?" Yes, Google hired Ray Kurtzweil to run their AI division.

Several weeks into his onboarding, he gave a presentation on Google's advances in AI and machine learning during a company-wide meeting. Knowing that he had the Herculean strength of Google's computing and programming resources behind him was surreal, inspiring, and formidable.

ANALYZING AMAZON

Perhaps no company; not IBM, not Google, nor anybody else affects all industries quite like Amazon.

Think about the breadth of their services. Besides their obvious megalithic website and other big ventures like Amazon Web Services (AWS) and Amazon Studios, they're breaking into groceries with Wholefoods, financial services with Amazon Pay, and healthcare where they may disrupt everything from the pharmaceutical supply chain to Medicare management. Soon, there won't be an industry available in which they don't have a presence, or even dominate.

Further proof that there are many different ways to succeed, Amazon's organizational approach is a stark contrast to Google. The workspaces at Amazon's Day One building are meant to symbolize how far they've come and how far they still have to go. It's a no-frills work environment with simple desks meant to replicate the lore that Bezos used a scrap door for his desk when he started the company. The office—as a whole—had a scrappy startup vibe within a corporate behemoth preparing for many years of explosive growth.

Reading recommendation: The Everything Store by Brad Stone. This book provides as in-depth of a look into the company as you can get without actually working at Amazon.

When I worked at Amazon Advertising (then known as Amazon Media Group), the company had around $500 million in revenues, but there was little known about the incredible scope of their advertising efforts. Of course, the main website was a giant piece of that, but there was so much more. They also had a host of other websites like IMDB, Audible, Zappos, and others.

Amazon also has connected devices like the Fire and Kindle to leverage for advertising space. Then, the Amazon advertising platform allows people to buy against Amazon data anywhere on the web.

The reason this combination of technologies is so interesting and unique is that it ties into the merchandising arm of Amazon, where American legacy organizations like General Mills and Proctor & Gamble work with Amazon's vendor management teams to sell their products.

It's an interesting dichotomy that Amazon, a company with laser-like focus on creating the future, managed to convert more traditional merchandising concepts into digital activations for brands large and small on its product pages. It was less about building something brand new and more about innovating on a platform of ideas that wouldn't change, including their famous management principles. This situation also illustrates the certainty that customers always want more choice and lower prices—a conviction their leader, Jeff Bezos, captured in his flywheel on growth, which I'll discuss in chapter 5 about how to use frameworks. Unlike Google, Amazon creates the future around their core tenants and/or beliefs about things that won't change.

Amazon excels with tried-and-true organizations like Proctor & Gamble, while having their feet firmly planted in the future. For example, not long ago they bought Kiva—a robotics company that helps to automate their warehouses. They also have plans to use drones all over the world to deliver packages. By the time you're reading this, a drone may be heading to your home in less than three minutes with your new shipment of coffee pods, batteries, and dishwasher liquid, among an entire marketplace of other possibilities.

You just never know when Amazon is going to unveil something truly revolutionary. For example, I read an article in 2014 that mentioned Amazon had invested $100 million to support companies building upon its voice recognition technology called Alexa. At the time, I remember thinking that was a massive amount of money to dedicate toward what was then an unknown technology. Yet, nobody was talking about it much, and I couldn't understand why.

Now, it seems possible that Alexa will become known as *the* voice operation system of our time. In his last shareholder letter, Bezos wrote that there are now more than 150 different products available with Alexa built in, from headphones and PCs, to cars and smart home devices, and "much more to come!" From those 150 available products, more than 100 million Alexa-enabled devices have been purchased. That is a mind-blowing level of market dominance for the Alexa ecosystem. Best of all for Amazon, you can't get closer to a customer than their voice. At least not yet.

If you're staying on top of a company like Amazon, you'll be able to leverage that knowledge to stand out among the crowd of salespeople who continually walk in and out of a client's office. Your client won't remember the cavalcade of characters who came in asking them questions like, "So, what are your plans for next year?" or, "How can I convince you that our product is better than anybody else's?"

Most clients are tired of questions like that. You're much more likely to separate yourself if you come into their office and open a conversation with, "Hey, have you seen what they're doing at Amazon right now?" In that case, they're much more likely to remember you as the salesperson that opened their eyes to the latest world-changing plans at Amazon and how you can help.

Whether you're researching the way Amazon infuses advertising into its massive e-commerce operations or how they plan to infiltrate the modern world with robots, drones, and tellerless stores (e.g. Amazon Go), you can't go wrong if you take a deep dive into what's late-breaking at Amazon. You just might uncover the next great disruption your client will face in their industry before they do.

Game Changer #10: See how Amazon and other industry leaders are investing their money. This can provide early insight into the next great technology you could be discussing with clients.

ALL ABOUT ADOBE

Google, Amazon, and IBM are names that are immediately recognizable as having a massive technological impact. Don't underestimate the impact of Adobe, however, in your efforts to ramp up on technological trends and industry influence.

There is much more to Adobe than PDFs and Photoshop. Not only does Adobe own the world's leading document solutions software and the world's leading suite of creative technologies (all of which can be accessed by subscription via the cloud), it also offers market-leading enterprise technologies.

Adobe's lesser-known division called Digital Experience covers everything from digital analytics, to advertising and commerce, to campaign orchestration. This places Adobe at the center of powering massive digital transformations occurring at nearly every major company on the planet. The goal is to provide customers with the capacity to create immersive digital experience across all channels, seamlessly and with real-time personalization.

By the time I joined Adobe, I had already worked for some incredible companies that are doing amazing things. Still, this company managed to raise the bar for its enriching professional environment.

On my first day, I sat at a large, horseshoe-shaped table with around fifteen of my peers on the forty-third floor of our office in Times Square. The talent around the table was quite impressive, whereas I could tell right away that all these people were highly skilled. They covered the spectrum of Adobe's industry groups—retail, travel and hospitality, media and entertainment, education, financial services, and other key strategic verticals.

It was a cold evening in late January. I could see the sun setting across the cityscape, which provided an inspiring and uplifting backdrop to do great things. We were in the meeting for a weekly conference call concerning our first quarter pipeline. The goal of the discussion was to cover the top ten or so deals across the team, with our VP and others around the country who dialed in to the meeting from various remote locations.

As we discussed each deal, I noticed there were no flashy presentations or pomp and circumstance of any kind. It was all numbers and action, which was highly efficient.

I couldn't help but feel encouraged that every team member was there to assist each other. Being a newbie, I was especially glad to see this. Everyone was welcoming and offered their assistance to get me up to speed. There was an innate sense for genuine camaraderie across the entire sales team.

I quickly noticed Adobe created a standout corporate culture based on a thoughtful and clear set of values, perhaps more effectively than any other company I had previously worked for. Although Adobe isn't as well-known as some of the other companies in this book, I'm highlighting their values because they're what make Adobe a special place to work.

Adobe's values are to be genuine, exceptional, innovative, and involved. Those four principles guide the behaviors and expectations of everyone working at the company. As such, Adobe's team members, in all areas of business, live and breathe those values every day.

Based on the definitions of what each of those values mean, the company encourages a deeper level of involvement with clients and the community alike, which has always struck me as particularly impressive.

For instance, not only does Adobe strive to know a client's business inside and out, in an effort to move past immediate considerations and build long-term partnerships, the company also maintains a strong presence in the communities in which it operates. Adobe employees hold numerous events to engage the local community and make concerted efforts to generously donate their valuable time as well.

The company has experienced significant growth over the last several years. In 2017, Adobe generated about $7.3 billion in revenue. At the time of this writing, the company currently holds around 4,300 patents and is forecasting over $11 billion in revenues in 2019. With that type of growth and industry impact, Adobe is definitely worth your time to research.

An especially attention-worthy item for your consideration is Adobe's highly active acquisition history and go-to-market strategy, a key factor that enables Adobe to set the standard for digital experience technology. This is a lesson to be learned by analyzing almost any enterprise-level company. Adobe, however, happens to be especially good at acquisitions and has acquired many companies, so it's easy enough to do some quick research on this aspect of their success.

35 Years of Adobe Acquisitions & Product Evolution

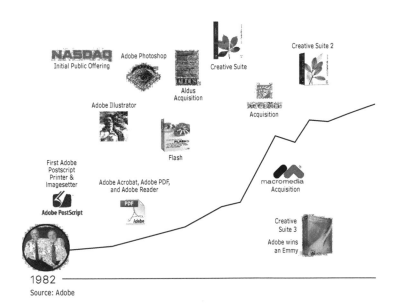

Source: Adobe

Looking at a company's acquisition history is a valuable piece of information for any salesperson because it helps you to understand what their future bets are and in which direction the business is going. If you find a company that regularly executes acquisitions, you might find some gaps in their portfolio that could help you to discover a major area of need (or purchase) that will arise soon in their future.

Game Changer #11: Take some time to investigate the acquisition history and especially recent acquisitions of industry leaders. This will give you a full picture of their go-to market strategy and insight into what they're likely to do next.

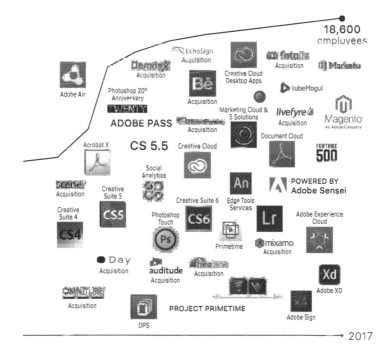

LEVERAGE YOUR KNOWLEDGE

Acquire a clear sense for the leading organizations in your industry vertical and follow Google and Amazon at a minimum. Write some notes about each one on a Word document or piece of notebook paper somewhere if it helps you to remember. Ask yourself some questions about their operations:

- How do they tie everything together?
- Are they focused on an all-encompassing marketing concept?
- What kind of language are they using?
- Is there a specific approach they use to bring products and services together?

By pondering questions like these, and any others you can come up with, you'll have a target for your research and it's likely you'll uncover a plethora of information. Consider books on technological change by prominent thinkers and business leaders, as well as analysts' reports to round out your knowledge base.

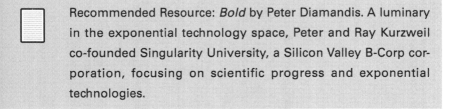

Recommended Resource: *Bold* by Peter Diamandis. A luminary in the exponential technology space, Peter and Ray Kurzweil co-founded Singularity University, a Silicon Valley B-Corp corporation, focusing on scientific progress and exponential technologies.

Geoff Ramsey (co-founder and CIO of eMarketer) delivers the most insightful, data-packed presentations you'll ever see on digital channel use and investment. Here's what he had to say: "Selling opportunities are always improved when you have the right credible information at your fingertips before engaging with clients or prospects. If you have the insights and data to back up where consumers are spending their time and money, and you know where companies and brands are spending their marketing dollars across digital and traditional channels, you're going to have a strong leg up on the competition."

Game Changer #12: eMarketer is a must-read if you are in the digital space. Analyst reports like Gartner and Forester are invaluable as well, because chances are that your clients are reading them to rank companies during their purchase decisions. If your clients are reading an industry publication, so should you.

SO...WHAT'S NEW?

Sales is like any other profession in one way: Sometimes we all need a figurative kick in the backside to keep pushing forward and breaking new ground. That sort of thing happened to me while I was working at Google.

I had become friends with Brian Cohen, co-founder and leader of the New York Angels (NYA), one of the world's largest group of angel investors. One day, we were sitting in my office at Google and he point-blank asked me, "What are you doing at Google these days in sales that's new?"

At his prompt, I explained all the happenings at Google and what I thought was special about our sales approach.

His reaction was underwhelming to say the least. In fact, I think he said, "So what you're telling me is there's really nothing new going on at Google that's different than any other company?"

For a moment, I couldn't help but agree with him. There was plenty of intensity around the data, and our sales presentations were completely customized to each client with custom performance analysis and benchmarking, but I couldn't think of anything that was really new or special from a sales perspective.

It wasn't until much later—after he left—that I realized what I was missing about the latest and greatest from Google.

At least until 2008 and maybe a bit beyond, sales organizations were hard-pressed to integrate data from spreadsheets into Customer Relationship Management (CRM) tools.

Around the same time that I had that discussion with Brian, Google was actually implementing transformative technology around the collaboration of work documents that replaced the need for infinite email chains and updates to static files. The tools they created paved the way for massive productivity gains around pipeline analysis, ROI calculation, presentation outlines, and more to be updated collaboratively in real-time.

Google was a pioneer in that technology and our sales team benefited greatly from it in the early days. I didn't think of it on the spot with Brian because it had become so ingrained, natural, and foundational to the way I was working, I almost forgot it was there.

Once technology becomes widely adopted, it can become taken for granted. These days, it's hard to remember a time when collaborative document sharing didn't exist, but it really wasn't all that long ago.

As a result of Google being forerunners in document-sharing, our team was able to create a few McKinsey-quality presentations on a weekly basis, as opposed to the month or more it would take other teams from other companies. That was a large and distinct advantage.

I took that advantage for granted when I was talking to Brian. Some technologies become so readily purposeful, we forget how impactful they are until we have time to reflect on them later. Document sharing is just one example of this.

I guarantee we're all using various apps and browser plug-ins today that weren't available ten years ago, yet they pay substantial dividends in productivity. My advice is to be sure to stay up-to-date on not only the firms that produce the technology but the technology itself. Remember the more effectively you can use technology to streamline or improve your sales processes, the more money you can make.

Game Changer #13: Technology is a major factor in sales innovation. This includes advancement in sales tools and processes, which are instantly propagated over LinkedIn, embedded within CRM systems, streamlined in mobile apps, keystroked via browser plug-ins, and enabled through shared documents. Technology continues to drive automation into outreach, calendaring, and analysis.

THE SALES TECHNOLOGY LANDSCAPE

For an excellent graphical representation concerning the vastness of the sales technology landscape, including all the productivity tools available from various companies, Google "Sales Tech Lumascape."

Luma Partners is an investment bank, focusing on digital media and marketing. They created a marketing tool called Luma Landscapes to demonstrate their command of various industries. Of course, the one that represents sales technology is particularly relevant for our discussion, but there are many other useful Luma Landscapes for other industries as well.

Notice how Luma groups available sales technology. That framework provides the ability to quickly investigate many different companies to locate technology that can be useful to you, your team, or your company. From there, you can focus more intense research into leading companies from each area to enhance your knowledge of the tools you can apply.

By acquiring and/or following these resources, you can use real data and proven techniques to understand how the industry and consumers are moving.

Deeply understanding your customers is an important aspect in today's game of sales. This understanding comes from a genuine sense of caring to do what's right for all the stakeholders of a deal. By simply trying to do the right thing, everyone reaps the rewards. The next chapter discusses some detailed information about how to leverage this mutually beneficial mindset to open new pathways to bigger and better deals.

CHAPTER 3

DARE TO CARE

"Nobody cares how much you know, until they know how much you care."

—THEODORE ROOSEVELT (26TH PRESIDENT
OF THE UNITED STATES)

When I go to a client meeting, I'm usually not the smartest person in the room or the most tech-savvy. On most occasions, I'm far from the most senior, and I often meet with VPs, SVPs, and occasionally, C-Level executives with teams of thousands under their wings. (Some of them run entire Fortune 100 companies.) Fortunately, I can make up for any gap concerning technical acuity, seniority, or just about anything else, simply by demonstrating how much I truly care for the betterment of my client's company and my own.

Over the course of my career, I've noticed this simple aspect of my personality has served me incredibly well and provided me with a huge advantage. Caring is a great way to level the playing field against competitors who may have more experience, knowledge, or even better genetics than you. Your level of caring has to be *genuine*, however. Anything to the contrary will be met with tremendous skepticism and ultimately, rejection.

Enterprise clients are some of the most intelligent and business savvy people in the world. They will sniff out empty platitudes and false pretenses in a heartbeat, but they will almost always respond favorably if they get a vibe for an approach that includes an expression of genuine caring to do what's right for their business, while both safeguarding and building their careers.

CARING SAVES

Despite your best efforts, things will go wrong in the sales process; it's inevitable. Occasionally, your customer's needs may change mid-stream. Other times, a highly anticipated feature release for a product may fall short of expectations, or a little used feature in general may be sunset, causing a disruption for your client's specific use case. There may be many other factors that can cause issues as well.

When those glitches occur, it will be invaluable for the client to know you have their best interest in mind. If they know that you care about the outcome as much as they do, all of those obstacles can be overcome.

Game Changer #14: Demonstrate your dedication and caring for your client's success early in the process by spending time to get ingrained within their business and focusing on how to drive results.

I remember a situation when I was working on a deal with a large insurance company. I was helping them to design a new approach to manage advertising operations. Their particular situation, however, was quite complex. They had a unique structure and requirements for internal collaboration between business units, which made for a situation I had never before encountered.

I took extra care in making sure there was nothing we over-looked in the new design we built. Unfortunately, my team and I missed something. Despite many implementations between us, none of us noticed a unique technical requirement that emerged, which prevented us from having a unique identi-fier flow through the system as we anticipated. This oversight required us to re-evaluate our delivery recommendations on a fundamental level, which would likely contribute to unwanted, increased complexity in ongoing operations.

The moment I realized that I overlooked something so crit-ical, my face dropped, and I felt a chill come over my entire body. "No way! I can't believe I didn't catch that," I said to myself. I double- and triple-checked our technical discovery, but it appeared there was no workable solution other than a complete redesign. Needless to say, I was more than a little stressed about the conversation I had to have with my client the next day.

When the time came to face the music, I walked into my cli-ent's office, ready to accept blame, apologize, and vow to do everything I could to make sure I fixed the issue without any unnecessary costs or delays. I had already notified both my management and internal teams about the potential issue we were facing from an implementation perspective. In addition,

I had tracked down several experts to evaluate the potential of the downstream impacts to the client's company and my own, as well as to provide recommendations for implementation alternatives. Yet, I was still bracing myself for an extremely agitated response, which would have been totally justified.

Much to my surprise, however, my client responded rather nonchalantly by saying, "Oh yeah. No matter what you do, there's always going to be a surprise of some sort. I understand. Don't worry about it. I'm sure we'll find a way to fix it."

Figuratively speaking, my jaw dropped, and my heart stopped palpitating. His response totally floored me. I visualized profanities being shouted, objects being thrown, and perhaps even getting escorted off the premises by security...

But none of that happened. Instead, he realized that I cared about him, his team, and his business. He placed significant value and faith in our partnership to overcome the blocker we had missed.

That encounter served as validation of the approach I had naturally applied for many years. It accentuated my belief in caring as an irreplaceable intangible in the salesperson's make-up and mindset. Obviously, if you don't have the right technology or price point, you'll be facing an uphill battle to close any deal. But if those things are equal, caring can be the key differentiating factor, and you can do that with no experience at all.

DO THE RIGHT THING

Caring certainly isn't something unique to me, and I don't

really consider it to be part of a methodology. But it is a seldom-discussed, common characteristic of many successful salespeople. Effective salespeople know when to challenge their clients by guiding them in a certain direction, but they also understand when it's time to stick their own necks out and advocate on their client's behalf.

There have been many occasions in my career when I've heard an account executive or sales manager say something like, "This just isn't going to work. Somehow, we have to make this right for our client."

A good example of that sentiment occurred several years ago, when I was working on a deal for a major credit card company with one of Adobe's top sellers, Steven Fay. Numerous issues (delivery shortfalls with technical implementation, a shift in strategic direction, ineffective campaign optimization due to third-party resources, and client-side product launch delays) had emerged. The sum of these problems was going to account for significant unforeseen expenses.

While we were collaborating on the gory details of how to address and fix all those issues, it would have been much easier for Steve and me to just let it go and say something like, "Oh well, this isn't really our problem. We're not the delivery team and can't be held accountable for client-side launch delays. Let's just send them a bill when the time comes and let someone else worry about it."

A lot of salespeople may have done exactly that. Unfortunately, it seems like some salespeople don't really care at all, which is a big problem, not only for their clients but also for the companies they represent and for themselves. They may not realize how caring builds goodwill, and how having a firm set of principles to abide by gives the client an invaluable peace of mind.

Clients place a lot of value in knowing that no matter what contract they sign, they'll never have to look at it again, because their expectations will be met or exceeded with fairness and integrity.

Steve and I were both innately driven by the long-term impact on our client's best interest and determined to help, even though we knew that corrective measures might result in a temporary revenue shortfall for our company.

We could have done the safe, easy thing and held the client to the contract without trying to help them at all. In the short-term, it would have brought in more revenue for our company, helped Steve and I to reach our quota more easily, and saved us a lot of time. But what would that have done for our long-term relationship with the client? It would have been extremely detrimental to our ability to secure future deals, and we would have burned the client on Adobe for years to come.

Instead, Steve and I went the extra mile for our client, even though we had other internal stakeholders consistently pressuring us to bring in more revenue elsewhere. We still knew that helping our client was not only in their best interest and ours, but it was also flat-out the right thing to do. I distinctly remember at least twenty occasions when Steve said, "We can't let this happen."

In the end, we worked tirelessly to do what was best for the client. To our surprise, it paid off with not only immediate business, but also with the long-lasting partnership we were hoping to build. In the end, that client became one of our company's top reference customers.

GREATER CLIENT SOPHISTICATION REQUIRES MORE COLLABORATION

The Digital Age has given today's clients a nearly infinite level of information at their fingertips and created buyers who are much more sophisticated than ever before. As a result, you need to be prepared that your clients may know more about how your solution integrates within their technology stack in the context of their business than you do. Often, you'll be in a situation where the client might have a decade or two more experience in your industry vertical than you. When you care about your clients, it becomes easier to do your homework by researching the industry leaders as I described in the previous chapter. There are a few key points to remember about that.

- Leaders and decision makers of today's companies are involved with the details of processes and systems like never before. Many of them have practitioner level understanding around deploying and managing technology across multiple platforms.
- Clients today are also much more focused on risk. Always be prepared to address any perceived risk they may have

with implementing your proposed solution. This includes risk related to their business goals, internal credibility, processes, implementation, ongoing services, legal issues, security, and more.

- The landscape of sales has become a client-side battleground in a lot of ways. This is a result of legal and procurement having significantly more control than they did in previous years. In a lot of companies, even the C-Suite executives may have difficulty overcoming pushback from either of these departments, especially in highly regulated industries.

All these changes in the sales environment add up to a more complicated sales cycle, which means you need to prioritize a consultative approach that stresses collaboration perhaps above all else. (More to come on your consultative approach in chapter 5 and beyond.)

 Game Changer #16: Caring will improve your collaboration, which will in turn add meaning and fulfillment to your work.

KNOW EVERYTHING ABOUT YOUR PRODUCTS AND SERVICES

I always try to make sure I know everything there is to know about my products and services. This ongoing quest for knowledge is driven by my level of caring for my company and the team, as well as a desire to deliver impactful results for my clients. Otherwise, how could I possibly serve my clients' best interest if I don't fully understand what I'm selling to them? That's why when I join a new company, one of the first things I do is attend a Quarterly Business Review (QBR), monthly sponsorship meeting, or whatever meeting has the most detailed information on what and how our company is delivering for a given client.

In one such meeting that occurred on a rainy day in Detroit, I observed a team of three account managers present an incredible package of research and consultative information to three or four client attendees. We were seated in an oversized conference room with a one-hundred-inch screen, where the account management team seemed to work in perfect partnership with each of the clients.

Reams of custom reports were presented about how our technology performed, the revenue growth strategies deployed, benchmarks about how our client stacked up to their competition across a variety of criteria, and crisply defined product updates and betas—each tied to a specific plan to deliver value.

That meeting gave me an immediate immersion into the results produced by our technology and personnel, as well as insight into how performance data was analyzed and presented. I witnessed, first-hand, what a successful five-year client relationship looked like, one that would likely last for another five years or more. In addition to giving me deep insight into the actual application of our products, this meeting provided me with an invaluable story to share with clients in the future.

Gaining a deeper level of understanding for what our software means for a top client was extremely beneficial for me. If you're new to the sales game, I recommend visiting with your team as they're making a similar presentation, or at least dialing into the conversation. The insight you gather will get you up to speed on the products and services you're selling much more quickly than operating exclusively via your own research. Furthermore, you'll come away with stories that will help you close because you'll have a crystal-clear vision of what success typically looks like at your company.

Game Changer #17: Reviewing static product documents and specifications is not as memorable or useful without seeing how products come to life for your customers. Only then, can you truly understand the product—what it is, what it does, and what it means for your customers.

EVERYTHING STARTS WITH CARING

Caring is one of many virtuous and helpful personality traits that are hardwired into all of us to some degree. Don't be tempted to shut it off in a singularly-focused effort to hit your quota. Rather, lean into caring as a wellspring of motivation and purpose, and as a checkpoint for client-centered decision-making. The outcome will be an intrinsically more collaborative relationship with your clients, and results will naturally become much easier to accomplish.

While caring is a key element of the foundation for which everything in this book is built upon, it is important to remember that your client relationship should not be used as a crutch. Caring is not a sales methodology. Therefore, it should not be thought of as a selling style on which to base your actions.

We'll talk more about selling styles later in the book. For now, just remember to tap deeply into one of the most human aspects within all of us—caring—but don't forget to use proven systems and frameworks to complement caring and other intangibles you naturally possess. That's where Part II will help, as it provides you with the foundational knowledge about those systems and frameworks to build a reliable and sustainable routine to make pipeline development automatic.

Game Changer #18: Consider caring to be the foundation of your sales success. It is the starting point that makes everything more achievable.

PART 2

AUTOMATIC PIPELINE

CHAPTER 4

PERSIST WITH A SYSTEMATIC APPROACH

"Persistence is the single biggest predictor of employee success."
—ERIC SCHMIDT (FORMER EXECUTIVE
CHAIRMAN OF GOOGLE)

When you create something that's simple, reliable, and effective, use it for as long as you can, because that is one of the rarest and most valuable commodities in any profession. I stumbled on that exact formula many years ago while working at IBM as a consultant, before moving onto business development.

At the time, the challenge was that I could only dedicate around a third of my time on the sales effort.

The assignment consisted of forming business development partnerships with mobile application companies—a company type that was brand new at the time—and telecom providers. This meant I had to create sales materials, demos, pricing, etc. from scratch.

In the early stages of the project, I had an excruciatingly difficult time trying to figure out how to track my next steps efficiently. My approach wasn't organized effectively. I was wasting far too much time on tasks that would have been much easier with a little structure on which to fall back. I was staying up late for too many nights just going over meeting notes. Overall, I was trying to drive too many actions around each opportunity. It was like trying to hit a grand slam with nobody on base.

After a conversation with leadership about the progress we were making, I had an epiphany. It struck me that I *needed* (not wanted) to find a better method. I *needed* a system to build pipeline, categorize deals, and qualify leads. More importantly, I *needed* a system with which I could develop automatic persistence.

The system I developed—and still use today—is so simple, it's almost laughable, but it's extremely effective. I've broken it down into four buckets for you to examine. Hopefully, it's enough to get you kickstarted into creating your own reliable approach. If not, give mine a try. I've shared this information with colleagues in the past, and just about all of them have raved about its effectiveness:

1. **The Pipeline Activator**—If you're starting a new role, taking on a different territory, or struggling to create opportunities, draft this simple spreadsheet and use it as a reference guide to kickstart or invigorate your efforts.

2. **The Opportunity Basket**—Breaks down your opportunities into smaller and larger deals and accentuates the importance of balancing your time to both categories. This is a mental model. Unlike the other aspects of this system, there isn't an overwhelming level of detail that needs to be written down. It's easy enough to track this internally.

3. **The Prioritization List**—A timesaving spreadsheet to help you locate the best deals among your list of clients. By spending a day or two on this task before engaging your territory, you'll optimize your time and energy.
4. **Begin by Visualizing the End**—Aligns your sales strategies with the contractual realities within your company, so you don't chase leads that aren't practical, overpromise things you can't deliver, or leave money on the table due to ineffective deal structure.

The sum of these four items equates to a system that will drive efficient, continuous action towards hitting your number right out of the gates and enable superior performance going forward. Otherwise, you will add significant risk to your efforts in at least four key areas:

- You could invest far too much of your time on the wrong leads at the wrong companies.
- You won't have a solid idea about what your commercial framework is, which could cause issues in how you position deals.
- You will likely spend a disproportionate amount of time on small or large deals, leaving one of them vulnerable to oversight, resulting in added risk to hitting your quota.
- You might waste time with the wrong individuals on the client side.

Later on, I'll tell you all about how I recommend handling risk, but there's no point in adding more of it, so implement a system that removes these easily avoidable threats. Then, you'll have more time and mental resources to handle the risks that are not easily prevented.

THE PIPELINE ACTIVATOR

Recently, I put my system to the test again when I took on a mix of old and new accounts at Adobe. I had reached my wits' end one night trying to build a pipeline of new opportunities while making existing deals happen. Eventually, I decided I needed a break, so I figured that binge-watching Netflix was a better investment of my time for the rest of the evening.

The next morning, however, my Netflix-inspired refresh appeared to have done wonders, and a solution to my problem became crystal clear. As I settled into my morning coffee, I realized that I had become so wrapped up in the recent changes to my list of clients that I had forgotten to input them into the system that had served me so well over the years. When change occurs—as it inevitably does—it's easy to get caught up and forget about some of the behind-the-scenes activities that drive success.

What a relief that moment of realization was for me. Excitedly, I opened up the template I used the year prior, updated it, and got to work with renewed optimism.

Within twenty-four hours of updating my pipeline-building spreadsheet, I was able to advance my entire pipeline across fifteen of my top accounts by simply listing the names of all my prospects and answering two basic questions:

1. Do I have access to the decision maker? (If the answer is yes, that's great! It's time to make some phone calls. If the answer is no, either reach out to the person in charge directly or find a different contact who could get you there.)
2. What is the last action I took, and on what date did it happen?

Not exactly rocket science, is it? I understand a lot of folks out there might be thinking, "Seriously? You're telling me that whenever I'm searching for sales leads, the answers to those two stupidly simple questions will solve all my problems?"

I know it sounds a little naïve, but responding to those two questions enables you to cease your anxiety over building a pipeline and get to what really matters. A system like this is so cut and dry that it takes the emotion out of the process. By leaning into it, you can't get sidetracked into a thousand different directions with no verifiable purpose.

You can update the spreadsheet as needed and refer back to it once or twice a week to make sure your primary focus is in the right place.

Perhaps the most magical thing about sales—in my opinion—is that the amount of time invested has nothing to do with the outcome. This system is a perfect example of that, because it allows you to achieve extraordinary results in a condensed time period.

PIPELINE BUILD				Target 3-5 Quality Meetings Per Week
Firm	Opportunity	Contact	DM*	Next Step
American Express	Opportunity #1	Dan	Y	Follow up to set next meeting
American Express	Opportunity #2	Angela	N	Try office and caller per assistant
American Express	Opportunity #3	Steve	N	Spoke with peer, intro needed
Google	Opportunity #4	Shelley	Y	Texted "Swamped"
Google	Opportunity #5	Bill	N	Last contact email
Proctor & Gamble	Opportunity #6	Amit	Y	Schedule challenges discussion
Proctor & Gamble	Opportunity #7	Donna	N	Discussed internal event
Proctor & Gamble	Opportunity #8	Rico	N	Set demo ASAP
LMVH	Opportunity #9	Rita	Y	Legal review
SAP	Opportunity #10	Akiko	N	Follow up
SAP	Opportunity #11	Emily	N	Follow up
etc.				

*DM = Decision Maker

Game Changer #19: It's a waste of valuable time to incessantly look up who to contact or decide what call to make next. Instead, create a reliable system that drives continuous action, test it, retest, and iterate over time.

THE OPPORTUNITY BASKET

The ideal pipeline should extend through several quarters and include the right mix of small and large deals.

Smaller deals are the ones you should be able to close with a standard go-to market strategy. They should be easy to support and fit tidily within your company's pricing model. Once you've gone through the sales cycle on a few of them, you should be able to follow the same process pretty closely on the rest, and little will change or surprise you along the way.

Ideally, you want to be progressing on one or two large opportunities at all times. These deals will involve a higher level of strategic, operational, financial, and/or legal complexity. Unlike the smaller deals, the larger ones might vary greatly from your company's standard go-to market model.

The larger deals will be the opportunities you need to exceed your quota and get noticed as a great salesperson. One important thing to remember, however, is that your level of focus on each client must remain consistent, whether they're considered smaller deals or larger ones. Otherwise, you'll risk throwing off the balance in your opportunity basket, which can make it difficult to maintain an effective pipeline in the long run.

Your opportunity basket should begin with a fifty-fifty allocation of your time spent between small and large deals. If you start to notice that you're closing larger deals a little more easily than you originally planned, you may be able to modify your time allocation to a sixty-forty mix in favor of larger deals. Likewise, if those larger deals are more complex than you suspected, you may want to shift the time invested in your opportunity basket to the opposite direction.

OPPORTUNITY BASKET

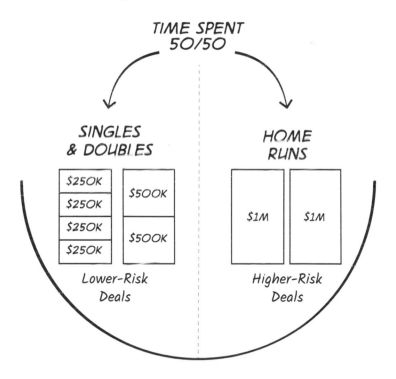

What does your Opportunity Basket look like and how much time are you really spending on Singles & Doubles vs. Home Runs?

If you don't reevaluate the mix of your opportunity basket every month or two, you increase the risk of misappropriating your time, which could lead to decreased efficiency and output.

Investing too much time in one large client is a risk-heavy scenario for a couple reasons.

1. If for some reason (perhaps even beyond your control) that deal doesn't close, you could miss your quota by a large margin. In that case, it's likely that not only did you not secure the big fish, but you also lost out on all the smaller fish by ignoring them in favor of a futile chase of Moby Dick. Consider this situation the Captain Ahab problem.

2. A potentially worse fate exists if you actually close that large deal and everyone thinks you're a hero... for the moment. What happens if you got so singularly focused on that client that you spent no time tending to smaller deals or building your pipeline? In that case, you're likely headed for a rather abrupt and painful fall from grace, because you may have severely limited or have zero opportunities on the horizon for the next month. In this scenario, you become yesterday's news rather quickly; consider this the one-hit-wonder problem.

The opposite problem can also take place. You might be able to knock down smaller clients like pins in a bowling alley. However, if you don't dedicate some time to a big fish or two, a herculean effort will be necessary to make your quota.

You may occasionally notice that a larger deal can be broken down into smaller, less complex, and more standardized blocks of deals. Similarly, smaller deals can sometimes be grown into much larger opportunities, which can be a tremendously satisfying process. It will always be much more difficult to ladder-up your deals than to ladder-down. More on that in chapter 12.

Another happy result of this method is that it prepares you for when problems arise. By conscientiously balancing energy in larger and smaller opportunities, you'll be ready for anything, because you've seen almost every type of situation that can happen.

If added complexity comes up, you'll be ready for it, because you've already participated once or twice in the big deal version of the game of sales.

You'll also be well-versed with the tactical demands typically involved with smaller deals. This will have given you solid practice with the mechanics of the processes at your company. When a larger opportunity arises, you'll be prepared to act with a skilled and knowledgeable approach.

Game Changer #20: To ensure you don't get overly focused on small or large transactions, create periodic checkpoints (perhaps every month or so) to ensure you're balancing your time properly.

THE PRIORITIZATION LIST

At the start of it all, you should spend a few hours qualifying your potential clients—analytically using a simple process that will save you an enormous amount of time and energy. In fact, this is the first thing you should do before you begin working a new territory.

This simple spreadsheet is composed of all the public and internal sources (systems, colleagues, intranet, etc.) you can draw upon for information to help you evaluate your list of prospects before you engage them.

When I started at Adobe, I had a list of around eighty potential prospects, many of which were Fortune 100 companies. Realizing that it wouldn't be possible to develop good relationships with all of them, I decided to create another spreadsheet; one that would rank and qualify them, analytically, into groups of favorability. I wanted to make sure I had all my ducks in a row before I talked to any prospects.

I began by listing out the companies and their base of operations. Knowing their location told me if they would be easy or hard to develop a relationship with, based on how far I had to travel to get there. Then, I wrote down some other variables, such as the budgets they likely had for each product set.

If the company had an existing set of delivery partners, but they didn't work well with us for some unknown reason, I knew pretty quickly that building a relationship would be an uphill battle at best. Therefore, I made a special note if they already worked with a friendly partner, because that would increase my odds right away.

Perhaps the most important piece of information on that spreadsheet, however, was whether or not the client already had an install of technology complimentary to mine. If the answer to that question was no, I knew right away that the chances of closing a deal would significantly drop, because the process of completely upending the client's entire architecture were low.

Drafting a spreadsheet that includes a list of qualifications is a tremendous time saver. Customize your spreadsheet to address the most important variables in your own company and keep it as simple as possible, because too many factors could add time to your already overcrowded to-do list.

Write down some key elements that describe what your optimal client looks like. Then, come up with a comprehensive set of potential blockers or deal killers. Without a good method for qualifying opportunities in place, you'll burn a lot of cycles by answering a constant influx of questions every time you get a request for information from an external source. Conversely, you'll save a lot of time if you can fill in your spreadsheet with the appropriate criteria, share it with your manager or a company veteran to review, and say, "I went through my territory to qualify it based on [insert your criteria here]... Here is how I ranked the companies in my list. Is there anything I'm missing?"

Client Name	1*	2*	Budget A*	Budget B*	Partner	Competition
Company 1	x	x	n/a	$11M	n/a	Competitor 1
Company 2	x	x	$25M	$50M	Partner 2	Competitor 2
Company 3	x	x	$22M	$10M	Partner 3	Competitor 2
Company 4	x	x	$20M	n/a	Partner 4	Competitor 3
Company 5	x	x	$15M	$20M	n/a	Competitor 1
Company 6	x	x	$10M	$2M	Partner 6	Competitor 2
Company 7	x	x	$7M	$1M	Partner 7	Competitor 3
Company 8	x		n/a	$20M	Partner 5	Competitor 2
Company 9	x		$6M	$20M	Partner 3	Competitor 2
Company 10	x		$6M	$30M	Partner 2	Competitor 3
Company 11	x		$5M	n/a	Partner 2	Competitor 2
Company 12	x		$4M	$13M	Partner 1	Competitor 3
Company 13	x		$4M	$5M	Partner 2	Competitor 3
Company 14	x		$3M	$2M	n/a	Competitor 1
Company 15	x		$3M	n/a	Partner 4	Competitor 1
Company 16	x		$3M	$5M	Partner 5	Competitor 2
Company 17	x		$1M	$1M	Partner 5	Competitor 3
Company 18			$30M	$40M	Partner 1	Competitor 3
Company 19			$25M	$20M	Partner 4	Competitor 1
Company 20			$20M	$10M	Partner 2	Competitor 3
Company 21			$20M	$7M	n/a	Competitor 1
Company 22			$18M	$1M	Partner 7	Competitor 3
Company 23			n/a	$14M	Partner 2	Competitor 1
Company 24			$5M	$5M	Partner 4	Competitor 3
Company 25			$3M	$9M	Partner 7	Competitor 1
Company 26			$3M	$11M	Partner 1	Competitor 2
Company 27			$2M	$2M	Partner 2	Competitor 1

This analysis has created three groupings of companies from the greatest amount to the least amount of opportunity. For example, in the bottom section, there is no complementary software installed. Therefore, these are not optimal prospects.

Legend

* Budget A, Budget B = estimate budgets for each of the two solutions you are selling.
* 1, 2 = types of installed software complementary to the products you offer.

When using a list like this one, I've discovered that I'm best off beginning my focused efforts with the top five to seven companies and working my way down from there. That approach is infinitely better than throwing a dart at the list and working on a company selected purely by random chance.

After you bring this list to review with others, you can collaborate on whether or not each opportunity seems to be worth pursuing. You can either proceed with the confidence of knowing you're spending your time wisely, or focus the bulk of your energy elsewhere if anything major was missing when you set your criteria. No matter what the result is, at least you'll have saved time and achieved peace of mind; two highly valuable assets in today's game of sales.

VISUALIZE THE END

After you've zeroed in on an individual client, you should visualize what the endgame looks like. You need to know the various terms of a typical contract at your company, so you can start to plan for what an ideal match between your offer and your client will look like at the end of a sales cycle.

If you've recently joined a new company or begun selling in a new territory, you should ask to see existing contracts. If you're part of a startup or selling a new technology and no existing contracts are available, sit down with the legal team and key executives to create a mock contract based on the legal necessities and pricing parameters around the business model.

I suggest uncovering related wins and reviewing executed agreements. Study the specific commercial terms of those deals immediately; because contractual details can be so unique that even a veteran salesperson might not be able to anticipate them. You need to know the perceived risk in the agreement from the client perspective, the real driver of price, sources of variability in how the terms are executed from license duration to implementation parameters, and how to maximize contract value for your company. Pursuing clients without knowing the specific terms of the contracts required by your company is like flying blind through a tornado of swirling variables.

 Game Changer #21: Track down the contract from a top deal, pour through every single detail, and visualize how you would go about arriving at the same with your prospects.

Imagine spending weeks of your time talking with an initial prospect and finally getting them to commit to closing a deal with you, only to find out that some contractual obligations from your company are going to make the deal impossible to close.

For instance, suppose your company requires a twelve-month committed license on all deals with no exceptions. What if you find out that the client you've been working with can only commit to a six-month deal? There could also be certain add-ons required for each agreement and many other legal variables could pose as blockers. If you weren't aware of those contractual obligations and didn't discuss them with the client beforehand, you have little chance of securing any deal between your company and theirs.

The old adage that time is money in the business world continues to hold true, even in today's fast-moving, ever-changing landscape. The last thing any salesperson wants to do is waste time chasing deals that aren't doable.

Reviewing agreements from recent wins gives you a precise visual of what you need to accomplish. You'll likely have one of two reactions, which is either, "Okay, that looks pretty simple. I can do this!" or, "Wow, I really need to dig in with legal, pricing, support, and some other things to get up to speed." Either way, you're tremendously better off and much more prepared than flying blind.

KEEPING THE FAITH

After you're prepared with the necessary spreadsheets and existing contractual information—whether you realize it or not—you'll have devised your own system. Test it, iterate it, and validate it. Once you've been able to vet that system by rapidly ramping up your pipeline a few times with no earth-shaking surprises, my advice is to place eternal faith in it and stick to it.

Going forward, you can easily tweak that system to adjust for changes in client buying behavior and the evolving technology landscape, but keep your faith in its foundational elements. Doing so will result in future compounded value, because it will save you time and enable more decisive action to create a virtual tidal wave of pipeline. Look no further than the reps around you who continue to dominate. Even if they won't share their secrets, rest assured that luck has *nothing* to do with their success. They're using simple, repeatable, and proven processes that you can learn and implement too.

The most artful way to establish your system is to find the right balance between pipeline build and execution. Be careful not to overshoot, because that can lead to mistakes.

Most salespeople are naturally inclined to worry too much

about building a big enough pipeline, but I caution against extending yourself too far. By taking on too much lead volume, you'll start scrambling in your execution, which can cause tremendous internal disruption. If there's too much on your plate, you run the risk of missing callbacks and ruining opportunities for future deals. You could also place unnecessary stress on delivery or product organizations, which can be harmful to your internal relationships.

Go through all the processes listed in this chapter and stick to your system religiously. Be sure to balance your time appropriately and you'll find the next level of success becomes a natural progression.

In the next chapter, you'll learn what some consider to be the secret to Amazon's enormous success. From that eye-opening realization, you'll discover how you can use proven frameworks to strengthen your own pipeline while becoming more consultative in the process.

CHAPTER 5

PERFECT FOCUS THROUGH PROVEN FRAMEWORKS

"I believe you need a diverse portfolio of viewpoints to see the opportunities others are missing."

—REID HOFFMAN (CO-FOUNDER AND
EXECUTIVE CHAIRMAN OF LINKEDIN)

As a result of my strategy consulting background, I strive to use, adapt, and create conceptual frameworks. Over the years, that sort of analytical thought process has served as an advantage, because it allows you to apply time-tested concepts to client interactions and deals. Various frameworks at the right point in time can be used to craft sales pitches, manage risk, and more. Knowledge of proven frameworks has become a practical way to amplify thought energy and direct activities. Now, I want to share that with you, so you can reap similar rewards.

You're probably thinking, "All this theory is great for an MBA Strategy 101 class, but I'm dealing with the cold, harsh reality of being pulled in a hundred different directions on any given day. I've got twenty meetings to attend this week alone; two hundred phone calls to make; and hopefully, a few deals to close. Who the hell has the time for frameworks?" You may not think you have the time, but to reach higher, you need to make the time. In this chapter, I'll show you the why, what, and how of proven frameworks, so you can implement them into your own routine.

THE FLYWHEEL

In an effort to convince you—100 percent—of how purposeful the right framework can be, I'd like to discuss one of the secrets to Amazon's success. Bezos himself credits a concept adapted from management guru, Jim Collins, called the Flywheel with helping him grow Amazon's business so successfully. Now, let's agree that if Jeff Bezos used this framework to generate billions of dollars in revenue at an astronomically high growth rate and created over a trillion in enterprise value, it's probably worth your time, my time, and just about anyone else's time to figure out how he used it. With that in mind, what is the Flywheel, you ask?

The Flywheel is an overarching framework for Amazon's business that makes management and strategic decisions much more consistent. For example, when the executives at Amazon asked themselves, "Should we build our own cloud computing infrastructure?" the answer was yes because they saw how it would lead to a lower cost structure, which feeds into lower prices—and it became one of the many facets of Amazon's growth.

Providing an excellent customer experience is where the

Flywheel—or as some at Amazon call it, the Virtuous Cycle—begins, ends, and continues (hence, the analogy to a cycle or wheel). By customers consistently engaging in positive interactions with Amazon, the company organically generates growth, which leads to lower costs and lower prices, which only enhances the customer experience, and on goes the cycle again and again.

Of course, this is an elementary overview, but it really is a concept that is exceedingly elegant in its functional simplicity.

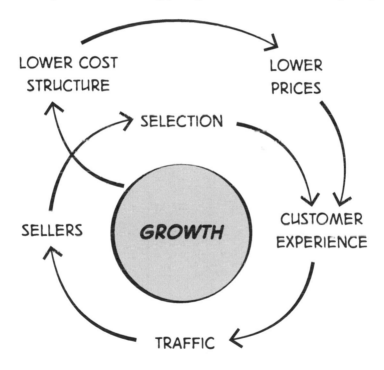

Recommended Resource: *Good to Great* by Jim Collins, author and management researcher.

THE MINTO PYRAMID PRINCIPLE

Amazon isn't the only example of an enterprise-level organization using a strategic framework to perfection. Strategy consultants at McKinsey use a different one called the Minto Pyramid Principle (MPP), which was detailed in a book by Barbara Minto in 1978.

MPP is orchestrated just the way it sounds. Start with a main idea or the solution to a problem. Group supporting arguments in three buckets beneath that initial solution. And finally, list additional supporting ideas beneath each of those.

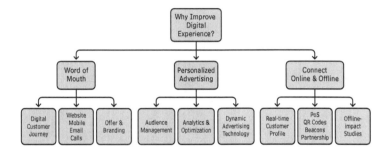

The human brain works in a hierarchical manner, so thinking about things in terms of the MPP is a natural, comprehensive, well-organized, and non-repetitive way to deconstruct complex problems.

Similar to my explanation of the Flywheel, I'm simplifying the concept of the MPP into a hierarchical approach. For a more detailed look at MPP, I definitely suggest checking out Minto's book. For now, understand that a hierarchical approach is a fast and efficient way to deliver recommendations to your clients.

Suppose you're in an elevator with the CEO from a top client for a few minutes, and she asks you point-blank, "What is your recommendation to improve our business?"

A good example of implementing a structured approach (depicted in the associated graphic) in this situation would be to respond with, "I've spoken with many people on your team, and everyone is focused on driving incremental growth as the most critical path to improve your business. I would suggest creating an improved digital experience, because that will drive incremental growth in three ways. First, it will generate positive word-of-mouth reviews. Second, it will yield robust data for more targeted and personalized advertising. Third, you'll be able to enhance your offline activities by supplementing them with digital data, which will tie online and offline engagements together to unlock new opportunities."

That *elevator pitch* would take you less than thirty seconds, yet it would deliver a powerful message to a key decision maker that provides an opportunity to greatly enhance their business, as well as your own.

Recommended Resource: *The Minto Pyramid Principle* by Barbara Minto.

Sure, *The Minto Pyramid Principle* was written in 1978, but the underlying concepts are timeless. After all, *Think and Grow Rich* by Napoleon Hill was written almost sixty years before that, and his book is still just as relevant today as it was then.

The Pyramid graphic is an excellent example of a business

framework, which you might not at first consider to be important in the area of sales. It's likely that your clients have MBAs or at least completed some form of management training. By knowing how to apply hierarchical thinking and business frameworks like Porter's Five Forces and the Boston Consulting Group Growth Matrix, you'll become more adept at engaging in strategic conversations with clients.

HOW TO APPLY FRAMEWORKS

Great frameworks aren't so much *created* by anyone as they are *discovered*. Investigate and test proven frameworks; modify or develop your own as needed. Then, pick the one that works best for your particular approach and stick with it. Before you can actually stick to anything, however, you'll need to know how to apply your chosen framework. To help you, I'd like to share a story from when I attended the Johnson School of Business at Cornell in an effort to become a strategy consultant.

One of the real-world applications I needed to pass while attending business school was a case interview.

WHAT IS A CASE INTERVIEW?

A case interview is a situational meeting where a candidate is asked to solve a somewhat typical business problem. The goal of such a scenario could be to answer a question like, "Why is the company losing money in Division X?" The candidate would then attempt to provide a logical flow of discovery questions and thought processes in applying proven frameworks to arrive at a potential solution. That recommendation will likely be backed up with high-level analysis based on experience from previous case studies or general business knowledge.

I struggled mightily with this task initially. My first couple of attempts in front of my peers were awful.

Practice made perfect in this particular situation, however. Even when my presentation was a mess in those first cases, I kept the visual of various frameworks in my mind. By going through case interviews with colleagues and friends over and over again, I became fluent in using those frameworks to articulate my points.

By around the tenth case I attempted with my classmates, I finally figured out how to apply structured thinking to systematically deconstruct the business problem and arrive at a thoughtful and well-orchestrated solution.

The moral of the story is to get a friend or, best case, a friend who does consulting work, and have them go through a few case interviews with you. Become adept at applying the frameworks you plan to incorporate and soon enough, your ability to deconstruct business problems and provide solutions on the fly will become immeasurably better.

Frameworks and systematic approaches can seem unnatural and appear difficult to apply at first. You need to resist any urge to ignore them, however, because they can increase your problem-solving ability by epic proportions.

If you come across a sales framework that is endorsed by your management team, you would be doing yourself a major disservice if you don't take it seriously and work diligently to apply it. You'll likely discover that there is an advantage to knowing the framework and applying it properly. Once you're comfortable with it, you'll be able to make the right decision around how much or how little to use it, or at what points in time the framework is most valuable to you.

Game Changer #22: Resist the urge to ignore frameworks as inconsequential, because they can add significant value to your skillset as a salesperson.

Game Changer #23: Practice makes perfect with proven frameworks.

There are many sales frameworks available that may suit your needs, but the one I endorse wholeheartedly is Value Selling®.[1]

VALUESELLING®

Developed by Lloyd Sappington while at IBM and later Xerox in the 1970s, (I'm starting to wonder if I'm partial to frameworks that were developed in the '70s) the strategic framework is widely used by top companies like Adobe, Salesforce, and Oracle, among others to support their solution-selling efforts.

At its core, ValueSelling® is a mathematical formula that focuses on minimizing risk to get deals done. It may seem a little overly analytical at first glance, but I've never seen anything as refined as this equation for enterprise sales.

---

1   The ValueSelling Framework®, Qualified Prospect Formula®, and ValuePrompter® are copyrighted
     © 2019 ValueSelling Associates, Inc.

The formula states that the Qualified Prospect® equals the Vision Match Differentiated times Value times Power times Plan.

$$QP = VM_D \times V \times P \times P$$

Qualified Prospect = Vision match differentiated x Value x Power x Plan

There's no need to get a headache over trying to figure out the math; all you need to know for this formula is that zero times anything is zero. The framework boils down to a simple set of conditions that ensure a prospect is qualified.

- You need to communicate a clearly differentiated offer to the client, where the client has a vision in their own mind around how your offer is the only one that can match their needs.
- Once applied, your offer will generate quantifiable value for your client over a specific period of time.
- You need to have access to decision makers of power.
- You need to meticulously plan the correct sequence of events—including procurement, security, legal, and any other reviews—through contract close.

If you're missing any of those elements, let's say you have a zero for "Plan," that means you have no qualified prospect, because zero times anything is zero. When applied, this structure can expose clear gaps and create an empowering level of confidence, because you know exactly what a qualified prospect should look like.

The most beautiful thing about ValueSelling® is that it promotes rapid and precise conversations among sales teams about deal qualification. It accomplishes this by placing a common framework concerning the key components of a deal into everyone's mind. That way, the team can rapidly collaborate on each individual bucket without missing any steps or falling down any rabbit holes.

Once you mention that your offer isn't differentiated in the mind of the client, the conversation can turn in a direction that addresses that shortcoming. In that case, the goal is to arrive at a vision of the future in your client's mind that only your company can deliver against. From there, the team can brainstorm potential solutions.

The ValueSelling® framework can be detailed in a document called the ValuePrompter®, which describes each element of the formula used to illuminate a sales cycle. An example of one of those elements could expose a gap that's formed because your team hasn't yet properly defined the client's motivation to accept your offer. This motivation could be corporate in nature or in the form of a personally vested interest. Ideally, the motivation would serve both purposes.

Most important, the ValuePrompter® is a great tool to guide your initial conversations and make sure you've captured a real solution for the client based on a solid business issue, which you can then share with the team. Otherwise, the client could think you went solo on creating a deal with zero follow-through, or you orchestrated a self-serving solution that didn't consider their best.

ValuePrompter® (example)	
CONTACTS	Rebecca, General Manager Sally, VP of Operations
BUSINESS ISSUE	Increasing growth and significant competition from alternatives to their core business line
ANXIETY QUESTION	If you don't have the technology to automate processes and reduce costs, how will your business and revenue be impacted?

PROBLEM	SOLUTION
Problem: Competition is preventing client from retaining the ability to service various regions, thereby reducing overall budget serviced and buying power, and increasing the rates they need to charge to be profitable, further exacerbating their decline **Problem:** Lack of control over execution and inconsistent technical setup across regions **Problem:** Lack of insight into what digital strategies are driving results	**Solution:** Leverage our technology to drive performance, eventually moving toward a managed service model to beat the competition, which is charging roughly 15% **Solution:** Create a unified buying platform across all regions while driving toward uniform technical setup **Solution:** Platform access for all to unify unknown to known data, map out, segment, and activate against customer journey

VALUE	POWER
Business Value: Increased performance by 10% across the board, thereby attracting new customers via competitive rates, enabled through cost reduction and streamlined processes, powered by our software and account management teams **Business Value:** time savings and strategic control **Business Value:** incremental sales by engaging customers across the funnel. Specific metrics to be determined **Personal Value:** Sally and the team feel that if they don't make changes now, they will continue to lose ground, which will negatively impact her job and advancement opportunities *Note: compelling event is our Q4 and current offer expires upon end of our fiscal*	**Rebecca:** key decision maker **Sally:** day-to-day, highly influential in acquisition of technology and contracting discussions **John:** Managing Director (Rebecca's boss), not likely involved **Ashley:** CTO, Sign off **Brett:** Procurement lead **Don:** Legal contact **Kim:** little involvement, sign off *Risk: pricing and budget could be a major factor, still*

PLAN
09/25 - In person discovery session 09/28 - Client sends budgets across all channels 10/22 - On-site strategy session 11/07 - Legal teams meet 11/16 - Client signs agreement 12/04 - Technical review and implementation 02/01 - Service commences 02/13 - Training on-site (date tentative) 03/25 - Summit event 04/05 - First Quarterly Business Review

Client & Partner Mutual Plan

Date		Action
Tuesday	25-Sep	In person Discovery Session
Friday	28-Sep	Client sends budget estimates
Monday	8-Oct	Client commercial parameters, draft Mutual Plan
Wednesday	10-Oct	Partner sends proposal
Tuesday	16-Oct	Client proposal feedback
Wednesday	17-Oct	Client exec review, feedback
Thursday	18-Oct	Partner set up as "vendor" in system, added to D&B, security check
Friday	19-Oct	Onsite visit plan
Monday	22-Oct	Onsite technical refresh, strategy discussion ▲
Monday	22-Oct	Legal council notified for upcoming agreement
Tuesday	23-Oct	Partner sends D&B number and Risk Information
Wednesday	24-Oct	Partner delivers Master Services Agreement, updated Partner agreement ($XMM Target)
Wednesday	24-Oct	Client team walks Master Services Agreement and agreement to Sr. Legal Council
Wednesday	24-Oct	Partner reviews Q&A with partner Implementation team
Friday	2-Nov	Client legal feedback, Partner sends updated agreement
Monday	5-Nov	Partnership strategy, overall cloud discussion ▲
Monday	5-Nov	Client approves legal agreement and Master Services Agreement
Tuesday	6-Nov	Implementation discussion, Reporting Demo
Wednesday	7-Nov	Controller meeting (date tbd) ●
Thursday	8-Nov	Risk & Security sign-off (date tbd) ●
Monday	12-Nov	Partner sends Certified Agreement, and Partner signatory name
Thursday	15-Nov	Signature process begins - Sally >> Rebecca >> Ashley
Friday	16-Nov	Partner signs >> Client signs agreement ▲
Monday	19-Nov	Partner provisions software
Monday	4-Dec	Pre-implementation discussion
Friday	1-Feb	Campaigns commence ▲
Wednesday	13-Feb	Onsite training (tentative date)
Monday	25-Mar	Summit event
Thursday	4-Apr	First Quarterly Business Review

Key Contacts & Roles

Client	Partner	
Sally, Advertising Team lead	Dave, Team lead	Steve, Account Management lead
Rebecca, Advertising Owner	Jane, Solutions Consultant	Katherine, Implementation Specialist
Terence, Security	Tim, Relationship Owner	Gina, Legal
Don, Legal		
Kim, Sr. Council		
Ashley, CTO and Signatory		
Libby, Controller		

Client & Partner Mutual Plan

Client Owner	Client Sponsor	Adobe Owner	Adobe Sponsor
Sally		Dave	
Sally			
Sally		Dave	
		Dave	
Sally		Dave	
Sally	Rebecca	Dave	
Sally			
Sally	Rebecca	Dave	
Sally	Rebecca	Dave	Tim
Sally			
		Dave	Tim
		Dave	Tim
Kim	Sally		
		Dave	Jane
Sally		Dave	Gina
Rebecca	Ashley	Tim	Ron
Sally	Rebecca		
Terrence	Sally	Dave	Jane
Libby	Rebecca		
Frank	Sally		
		Dave	
Sally	Rebecca		
Ashley	Rebecca		
		Steve	Katherine
Sally	Rebecca	Katharine	Tim
Sally	Rebecca	Katherine	tbd
Sally	Rebecca	tbd	
Sally	Rebecca	Tim	
Sally	Rebecca	tbd	Katherine

Legend
● new and critical Client action, dates tbd
▲ key milestones

Using the ValuePrompter® to unpack areas of need helps to get the client excited about working with you on a mutual plan. The mutual plan you create together will take all the information outlined in the ValuePrompter® and break it down into a much more granular level of detail that makes clear each associated action with the day it is scheduled to take place, as well as key contacts.

While in the process of writing this book, I had the pleasure of talking to Rick McAninch, a founding associate of ValueSelling Associates. I asked him, "What is the one thing you think all sellers can do better?" He responded by providing me with the following quote:

> "The ValueSelling Framework® is used by top enterprise sales organizations all over the world to accelerate revenue. While there are many powerful components of ValueSelling, such as the Qualified Prospect Formula®, the ValuePrompter®, and a detailed Mutual Plan to value realization, one thing I recommend all salespeople focus on in greater detail is clarity around the Business Issue. If you don't have a clear Business Issue, it will be nearly impossible to maximize value for your client and gain the support of senior management. Other initiatives that are connected to the core business issue will end up coming before your solution."

PROJECT MANAGEMENT

Doesn't it make sense that no matter what you do for work, you'd rather do it in half the time? If you were a warehouse worker, would you rather stock shelves for eight hours or four to get the same results? What if you were a customer service representative? Would you rather spend eight hours serving customers or four for the same impact?

Sales is no different. Why not reduce the sales cycle in half if you can make just as much money? Scratch that. Actually, by cutting the sales cycle in half, you'll likely double your income. Once you've identified what a good prospect might look like and get past the discovery phase, you can use project management to visualize—in your mind or on paper—how to accelerate the sales cycle. In fact, I would say applying project management to the sales cycle is a must.

To apply project management to your sales cycle, I suggest you first determine how many different activity streams, such as sourcing, legal, procurement, etc., you can operate at the same time. The more of these items you're able to parallel process without overwhelming your to-do list, the faster you'll accelerate the sales cycle.

In an attempt to keep project management at the forefront, you might ask some questions earlier in the process than clients may expect. Some clients may have an initial reaction of surprise and say something like, "Oh, I don't know if I'd even want to think about that sort of thing yet."

It's okay to get that sort of response though, because it still gets them talking and thinking about what's ahead. From there, you can get a feel for what dependencies or potential deal blockers may exist, and you can attack them before they present a serious problem or delay the deal.

I'm sure a lot of salespeople execute some form of project management even if they don't explicitly outline it. Some salespeople, however, may not realize how many things can be run in parallel, and inadvertently line up tasks end-to-end, leading to a much longer cycle with a linear, single-threaded approach.

Parallel processing in this way can accelerate your sales cycle so much that it could be the difference maker in meeting or exceeding your quota because you'll be reducing the cycle on each deal. Instead of getting four deals done, you might be able to close ten, maybe more.

SALES PROJECT MANAGEMENT FRAMEWORK

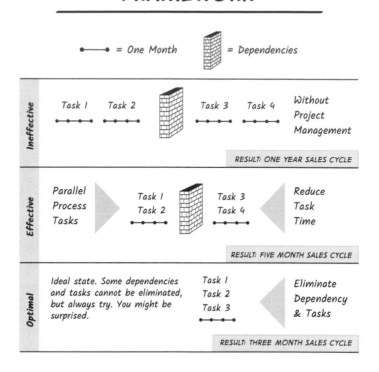

Are you project managing your sales cycles by parallel processing tasks, reducing task time, and eliminating both dependency and tasks?

THE TIME HORIZON

There are so many different frameworks you'll come across over the course of your career that it's not useful to explain all of them, but I believe the sales frameworks I've mentioned here to be the most important. The last framework that's worthy to mention is the Time Horizon, which is a mental model I use to make sure my client conversations aren't too focused on the short-term. It also concerns how you're thinking about the timing of what you're looking to offer the client, in relation to the client's perspective and their own time horizon.

This is critical because when you're out there searching for opportunities and trying to get deals done, it's understandable to feel the pressure of the moment. It's easy to get laser focused on getting deals done as soon as possible.

The unfortunate byproduct of that is, it's a total turnoff for the client. It's like proposing marriage to someone on the first date...at Arby's. You may think it's a great idea because the other person is incredibly attractive, smart, funny, and has a great family. But the object of your affections may want to take things much slower...or escape through the back door.

I really started to zero in on this framework after I misaligned my time horizon with one of my clients. It turned out that she was sitting across the table in a meeting, thinking about a three-to-five-year plan while I was talking about what we could do next month. Unfortunately, it didn't occur to me that our timing wasn't in sync, which prevented me from considering how we could support her strategic plan.

That misfire on my part taught me a valuable lesson. It showed me how implementing a framework around the time horizon was a critical part of the sales cycle for me.

Think about the timing of the sale from the perspective of your client. It may be years before they see the value they're looking for, because they'll need to ramp up on process and technology. Match this time scale early on by dedicating around 50 percent of your client-facing time to discussing what will happen in the first month, or maybe even the first quarter. Then, spend at least 25 percent of your time talking about what will happen in the next six months. From there, make sure you address the next year or two.

(X) TIMELINE

X = DISCOVERY × STORY × PLAN × VALUE

Illustrative time allocation, think critically about what yours should look like.

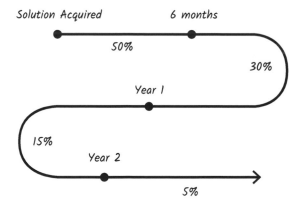

- *How much time are you spending selling to your future-state vision?*
- *Are you aware of your client's time horizon?*

It doesn't always occur to us that many of our clients may have been in their jobs for fifteen or twenty years and their companies could be one hundred years old. Therefore, they're accustomed to thinking about business partnerships that extend well beyond the first month or quarter. Their time horizon is vastly different from the average salesperson who focuses an inordinate amount of time on what is happening right now.

"Our clients have one foot in the past and the other in the future."
—JIM LECINSKI (FORMER VICE PRESIDENT
US SALES AND SERVICE AT GOOGLE)

It's easy for salespeople to forget to have conversations with their clients beyond the first six months of a deal. It's human nature to some degree to pay less attention to items that are past their point of urgency. Unfortunately, deals can run into issues as the result of an "out of sight, out of mind" oversight.

The key takeaway from this chapter is that there are many different frameworks that can be effective. Explore them all and use them effectively in conjunction with the reliable systems you learned about in the previous chapter. If you get especially good at implementing these techniques, opportunities for bigger and better deals, at a more rapid pace, should start to surface. You may begin to achieve your quotas more easily, start making more money, and achieve any other personal goals you were looking for when you first picked this book up.

Understand, however, that even with the best systems and frameworks clicking on all cylinders for you, serious challenges will present themselves. Occasionally, meetings will go south, the Dark Side of Sales will call to you, and painfully tough conversations will surface. Continue on to the next section to learn how to best get through all of it.

PART 3

UNSHAKEABLE RESILIENCE

CHAPTER 6

THE CERTAINTY OF HORRIBLE MEETINGS

"I've missed more than 9,000 shots in my career. I've lost almost 300 games. Twenty-six times I've been trusted to take the game-winning shot and missed."

—MICHAEL JORDAN ("HIS AIRNESS," AND
SIX-TIME NBA CHAMPION)

It's difficult to pinpoint exactly how many meetings I've had at this point in my career, but I would guess that number to be upwards of several thousand. Some have been excellent; others have indeed been horrible. Good results or bad, lessons were learned from just about all of them.

There was one particular client (a giant in the financial services industry), who I had two totally opposite meeting experiences with.

GOING FROM GOOD TO BAD

The first meeting was the stuff of which legends are made. It was a one-on-one lunch with a senior executive who had full budgetary control and operational ownership of marketing and advertising teams, partners, and agencies, so I was definitely talking to a decision maker. The lunch took place at an upscale, trendy steakhouse near the company's headquarters in New York City. The meeting was supposed to last about forty-five minutes, but it went on for over two hours because we had such a great back-and-forth conversation about how we could work together.

We talked about her company's entire digital operations and mapped out the organization, partners, budgets, planning cycles, and their technology stack to create a comprehensive plan that provided solutions to most of their existing problems. Both of us were extremely excited about the potential of forming a promising, new partnership, so we scheduled another meeting for one month later to get additional team members from both companies involved. Many of her colleagues were going to fly in from all over the country to attend as well.

The second meeting, however, was a complete whiff; the kind of strikeout where you see nothing, hear the pop of the ball as it hits the catcher's mitt, and then swing.

On the date of that scheduled follow-up, a snowstorm wreaked havoc on the Northeast and made it impossible for key players from both teams to attend. I was pretty upset about that because that first meeting went so well, and I wanted to carry some momentum into this one. Unfortunately, Mother Nature wouldn't cooperate, so we had to reschedule for another month later.

Strike one...

The second attempt for a follow-up meeting never happened either. Apparently, the client's team needed to schedule a last-minute off-site meeting on the same day.

Strike two...

A month and a half later (about one hundred days after the promising initial luncheon), the meeting was actually about to happen. Finally, there were no weather-related cancellations and no conflict with a mysterious off-site meeting. Another problem, however, presented itself. The admin who double-booked the last meeting attempt sent my invite with a meeting time that was thirty minutes later than everybody else's. As the organizer, I didn't think anything about it because I confirmed everything over the phone.

Strike three...

That was only one out and any baseball fan knows that each side gets twenty-seven outs in a nine-inning game. Therefore, it was time to dust myself off and get back in the batter's box.

Luckily, I always plan to show up about thirty minutes early anyway, so I was only a few minutes late. Nonetheless, I expected to arrive to a mostly empty conference room with plenty of time to organize my material and prepare for the meeting. Much to my surprise, however, the presentation was already on the screen and everyone was seated and ready to go. I had to hit the ground running, which put me in a totally different mindset and threw me off my game just a bit.

I soldiered on with my presentation, but several minutes into it I realized that it was probably just about the worst thing I was ever a part of. A quick scan of the expressions on the faces in the room and I realized I wasn't alone in that opinion.

When we got to the validation point of the presentation, the client seemed a little exasperated. She sat up straight and informed us, "Yeah, over the last several weeks, we worked everything out with our partner. Honestly, they've done an incredible job of turning things around and solving our problems."

You could almost hear the air being sucked out of the room at that point. All of a sudden, what was once a promising prospect that I was excited about three months ago now seemed like an exercise in futility. All was not lost yet, however, as she followed up her deflating statement with a gesture of consideration, "But let's see what you've got for us anyway."

Undeterred, I finished my portion of the presentation and handed it over to a solution consultant on my team, who put together gorgeous visuals of what their technology stack looked like against what it could be if we were to help streamline it with our solution. It included data flows, logos of the existing footprint based on our initial discussion, different inventory sources for their digital advertising efforts and more. It was clear that she customized the entire presentation and put a ton of thought into it.

 Game Changer #24: Be flexible in your approach to meetings. Read the room for reactions to your presentation. If the client doesn't appear to be responding favorably, be prepared to shift the conversation appropriately.

In fact, she may have actually put too much work into it, because her slides were so detailed that it got way too far into the weeds and the client began to lose focus, which was made quite clear when one of them blurted out, "So ... where's lunch?"

"I thought we were going out to lunch," I responded.

"Nope. We were told that you had arranged for lunch to be delivered."

Evidently, the lunch plans were also miscommunicated.

Let's take a quick inventory of the meeting variables at that point:

- One cancellation due to a massive snowstorm.
- A second cancellation due to an urgent offsite meeting.
- A lack of punctuality on my part.
- No more known problems to solve for the client. (Clients can always improve their business, regardless of how happy they are. I'm sure this client still had issues, but they either changed or we didn't know what they were.)
- And now, no lunch.

Other than that, everything was absolutely perfect!

The remainder of the meeting was mainly a formality. Once all the other mishaps were compounded by a room full of hungry people, a guest appearance from Beyoncé wouldn't have been able to sell that deal.

Obviously, that meeting was horrible. In fact, one of my

colleagues approached me when it was over and not-so-reassuringly told me, "Wow, that was a total train wreck! I'm glad I've seen you kick ass in a lot of other meetings. If I hadn't, I'd be seriously concerned about you."

In my head, I was thinking, "He's not wrong."

Ironically, that meeting—as horrible as it felt—served effectively as an important alert that I had gotten off-track. I needed to figure out why I had made mistakes that I normally avoid. Rather than lament its existence, I searched for lessons I could learn and changes I could implement to ensure I didn't repeat the same missteps.

 Game Changer #25: A horrible meeting could be the sign of a broader issue affecting all of your sales cycles. When this happens, take some time to assess and adjust immediately.

Thankfully, that meeting reinforced the importance of accountability, resilience, and control in my mindset. I already understood how crucial those things are, but for whatever reason—maybe it was the snowstorm or unrealistic expectations from a great first meeting—I neglected them. Now, it's up to me to ensure I never overlook these three critical sales' aspects again.

ACCOUNTABILITY

This was a painful reminder about the crucial nature of accountability, the lack of which resulted in that horrible meeting. It would have been easy for me to throw the assistant under the bus for the timing mishaps and lunch plans confusion, but that wouldn't benefit anybody. Given how things were going, it was my fault for not triple-checking the logistics.

In fact, it's embarrassing to admit the oversight. I should have never let being stretched out a bit too thin prevent me from digging into the logistics and engage in the client relationship a little further.

RESILIENCE

That horrible meeting highlighted how important resilience is. It would have been easy for me to wallow in the aftermath of that meeting. Sure, I experienced a moment of acute disappointment, but I made the necessary adjustments and moved on. In hindsight, I also noticed that I was tracking too many cycles that particular month.

Resilience is an essential part of every salesperson's makeup. When horrible meetings surface, I suggest calling upon that ability to shake off the experience and maintain a positive outlook about your next opportunity. Horrible meetings can also provide a good checkpoint for you to regroup and rework your plans.

CONTROL

I was reminded of the fact that there are some things that are simply beyond my control, and it's not worth my time to get caught up in them. For example, I couldn't do anything about the snowstorm delaying that initial follow-up.

By the time we had the meeting, the client's external agencies and partners had already solved a lot of the problems I planned on addressing, which was a 180-degree turnaround from the original meeting that caught me by surprise. My only recourse was to put together the best presentation I possibly could. Much to my dismay, it just wasn't enough to make up for all the changes that had snowballed at that point.

One more lesson, I also saw—firsthand—what happens when you miss on lunch. I always knew it was important but never missed on it before, so I never fully realized how critical it is. Whenever a room full of people can determine your fate, never let them go hungry. I feel like there's a Snickers bar commercial in there somewhere...

EVALUATION

Think long and hard about your career of meetings. Do any of them resemble the one I just discussed? Okay, maybe it didn't quite meet the perfect storm of dysfunction like that meeting did (or it could have been much worse), but if you've ever had one or more meetings where you could feel things fall apart before your eyes, congratulations! That means you've gained some invaluable experience to help you going forward. Keep in mind, there could be a variety of reasons for this experience.

- You might have over-extended yourself or your resources.
- Perhaps you weren't engaged enough with your client.
- It's possible that you were still refining your system for uncovering qualified sales opportunities. If that's the case, chalk it up as a valuable learning experience.
- Maybe you had too many cycles going at once.
- A reorganization could have distracted you.
- You may have suffered the inevitably human momentary lapse of motivation or focus.

If you look back on your meeting history and don't think any of them classify as horrible or even slightly off your game, you should solicit feedback from clients and teammates, and ask yourself some questions as well:

- How can I be sure I've never had a horrible meeting?
- If I'm really running perfect meetings, could I be running more? Am I pushing the envelope?
- Could I have accomplished more in the meeting? Did I aim high enough?
- What surprises—positive or negative—have I encountered during my meetings? Could I have anticipated any of them? Did I effectively leverage the surprises?

It's certainly possible to go through a long and happy sales career while having horrible meetings now and then. When you endure these un-highlights from your career, rest assured that you're not alone. I've had plenty of them and so have the vast majority of the greatest salespeople I've worked with. The key is to not let them get you down and learn as much as you can from each one. It's essential to understand why they happened.

Game Changer #26: Revisit any horrible meetings you've had in the past. Think about how you can hold yourself accountable and improve your approach to build better habits to prevent similar missteps from happening in the future.

PREVENTION

Despite the silver lining of learning experiences that horrible meetings can offer, nobody *wants* to have a horrible meeting.

I'm sure nobody has ever been talking with a teammate before an important client meeting and said, "I really hope this meeting goes horribly wrong, and I blow the deal for the whole team." With that in mind, I think there are some things you can do to avoid having horrible meetings.

- Priorities can change over time. No more than one week before the scheduled meeting, you should revalidate your agenda to ensure you're still aligned properly with the expectations of all attendees.
- Internally, ensure you research the client, attendees, and backgrounds thoroughly. You should also cover the roles and responsibilities for each team member and ensure everybody is clear about the desired outcome.
- Avoid—at all costs—jumping into your pitch right away. Even if the client pressures you to "get to the point," you need to prove to them that you understand their challenges first. Accelerating the meeting too quickly can result in the client not taking you seriously and shutting the door on you forever.
- You should also avoid talking prematurely about price. You need to understand your client's needs and discuss the value your solution can deliver first. You risk losing the client's interest immediately if you talk too soon about price, even if they ask for it. In that case, they may only be thinking about you in terms of, "How much is this going to cost me?" Rather than, "What is the value this partnership can deliver to my business and to me?"
- Ask open-ended confirmation questions throughout the meeting (e.g., "What did you think about X?) You don't want to do all the talking because the client will lose interest and you won't learn anything. This is an important way to keep them engaged during the meeting. As we discussed

in chapter 3, listening to clients wants and needs and anticipating the questions they will ask is integral to displaying a genuine sense of caring. This helps you to more carefully read the situation and customize your approach to meet your client's needs. The best salespeople have a combination of dogged determination and a refined ability to understand the motivations of others.

> **Recommended Resource:** *Secrets of Question-Based Selling* by Thomas Freese.

- Be mindful as you go through the PowerPoint slide deck frame by frame and be careful about sticking rigidly to the demo. If you've prepared well enough, you should be ready for anything, so be flexible enough to improvise, take questions, and even change the agenda if the feedback you solicit tells you it's necessary.
- Understand that the more senior an executive is, the more likely it is that your flow will get derailed. Be prepared to level-up your conversation to business issues based on what's happening in the room.
- When talking to your clients, keep in mind that you don't need to resolve everything in one conversation. Salespeople can feel pressured, wondering if they'll ever get another opportunity to meet with the client. When this happens, it's easy to push too hard, which could drive the client away, rather than engage them further in the relationship. Instead of trying to cram everything in one meeting, leave some issues open-ended to create time for both you and the client to come up with better solutions. If you execute

well enough on this initial meeting and don't come off as "pushy," you'll have plenty more chances to engage the client and achieve something that benefits all stakeholders.

- Book the next meeting before the current meeting is over and exchange contact information with all the new people in the room. This might sound like a no-brainer but it's easy to forget such a tactical step like this when you're focusing so strongly on your pitch and winning over the client.

Again, I'm aware of how important it is to not make all those mistakes because I've made every one of them at some point in my career.

GOING FROM BAD TO GOOD

Don't let the ominous nature of the potential for horrible meetings loom over you to create any negative energy, however. Allow optimism to prevail in your approach, because just as a great meeting can turn into a horrible one, a bad meeting can occasionally pave the way for a surprisingly great interaction.

I remember working with one client in particular, in which that situation took place. It came time to have a conversation with the procurement team, who completely dismantled the offer and pricing. They wanted to put the entire deal on hold and demanded to go to Request for Proposal (RFP), which would have not only picked apart the deal and elicited input from a number of different vendors, but also it would have delayed the process by at least six months. In other words, an unmitigated disaster was unfolding.

After that horrible meeting with procurement, some time

passed and because of all the great client-side work we had done, the client decided to work with us just as we had originally envisioned. The timing was right, and we achieved the executive-level access needed to turn things around for that deal. This was proof-positive that if you stay the course, work hard, and don't give in to finger pointing or allow negativity to overspill from one bad meeting or experience, things can take a turn for the better. That won't always happen, but meetings are just as likely to go from bad to good as they are the other way around. The key is to not let anything rattle you so severely that it takes you off your game. By the same token, don't allow yourself to become too overconfident, which could lead to overlooking some critical fundamentals.

At this point, I feel it's necessary to reiterate how rewarding and fulfilling the game of sales can be. Overcoming the challenging aspects, such as the near inevitability of the occasional horrible meeting, can be very rewarding. The knowledge that you're getting better with every meeting is not only encouraging, but it's healthy for your mindset. You just have to know how to most effectively deal with the perceived negative aspects of sales. Are they really even that negative at all? It's up to you to interpret each situation, calmly and rationally. Then, react appropriately to maintain your own happiness and success.

In the next chapter, I'll tell you how to handle the wider spectrum of challenges you'll encounter as a salesperson. I call it The Dark Side of Sales. It can be an ominous and solitary experience, but if you expand your knowledge base about how to deal with the challenges of a career in sales, you'll find your way back to the light much more quickly. May the force be with you.

CHAPTER 7

FACING THE DARK SIDE (OF SALES)

"Fear is the path to the dark side. Fear leads to anger. Anger leads to hate. Hate leads to suffering."

—YODA (JEDI MASTER AND MENTOR TO
TWO GENERATIONS OF SKYWALKERS)

Unless you suspect your father is actually a villainous half-man, half-machine bent on vengeance by destroying all that is good in the galaxy... facing the dark side of sales really isn't all that menacing.

There won't be any Jedi training with a small, greenish elderly creature, where you'll need to use your mind to make an entire aircraft levitate out of a murky swamp.

All *Star Wars* comparisons aside, the dark side of sales can present a difficult challenge that you're guaranteed to confront at some point, if you haven't already. Hopefully, by sharing some of my experience and insight regarding the dark side, the next time you find yourself in turmoil with it, you'll be ready for battle.

It was easy to see who represented the dark side in *Star Wars*. Start with the guy who's deep breathing and wearing all black. The dark side of sales is a little harder to recognize and may not be exactly what you'd expect. In fact, my informal definition for it is an unexpected happening that sidetracks your progress in a sales cycle, or even your job, something you weren't ready for, and you compound its impact by handling it poorly.   .

You may not see the dark side coming, but you can definitely feel it. It starts with decreased confidence. Soon after, your motivation and optimism may morph into cynicism. If left unchecked, it can lead to persistent unrest.

I've dealt with the dark side of sales several times, and I've seen nearly all of my coworkers face it as well. A few of them have succumbed to it for extended periods of time. The dark side creates an odd dynamic because dealing with it can seem like a solitary experience. Yet it is almost always there to some degree. We've all gotten sucked in for at least a brief moment or two at some point.

The dark side will present itself no matter how hard you try to avoid it. By reading about my experiences with it, you'll understand how to manage your expectations more effectively. You also might come to the full realization that things are likely going to be tougher than you expected. Most importantly, you'll be able to foresee issues starting to surface along the horizon of the sales cycle, which will enable you to become appropriately engaged.

At times, a career in sales can present some difficult challenges. But it is always an extremely rewarding and satisfying way to make a living. If it didn't require an expanded mindset of mental toughness and resilience, along with elite knowledge and a determined drive, sales wouldn't be one of the highest paid professions in the world.

My goal is to prepare you for when the dark side approaches, so you can minimize its impact, reduce the pain, maintain a positive outlook, and see the light. Once you've faced the dark side, eye-to-eye, you'll be able to more clearly focus on your success and appreciate all the reasons why sales is awesome once again.

The sage advice from the diminutive, green elder, Yoda, tells us that fear is the path to the dark side. That may be true in life ... and *Star Wars*. In sales, however, the catalyst for the onslaught of stress and anxiety seems to be a destructive reaction to uncertainty.

Uncertainty can appear in several forms, such as regulatory change, an unexpected earnings cap, the blame game, acquisitions and reorganizations, client misperception, internal competition, and even the natural ebbs and flows of business. We'll explore all of those areas, so you can see the consequences of the way you choose to manage uncertainty.

DEALING WITH CHANGE

While working at a startup, I faced unprecedented levels of change on a quarterly, even monthly basis. For example, the territories were constantly in flux. Once I became familiar with my clients and understood their needs, I was given a whole new list of prospects. That created a dynamic that made it beyond difficult to get into any sort of a professional groove, or so I thought, until I adjusted to the new environment.

The compensation structure was another area of change that consistently challenged me in that role. It shifted three times within a year and a half. While altering payout rules always made sense from a company perspective, and even benefited some sellers, they didn't align well for my personal situation.

Initially, that change in the way I was getting paid led me to a bad place but only for a moment. Rather than getting pulled into the dark side, however, I took immediate action to lay out the discrepancy and make a case to management.

Companies alter plans because it's the only way to remain competitive. How many companies have you heard of that had tremendous success by never changing? Also, companies usually implement change for good reasons, such as subpar metrics, decreasing revenue in a particular area of the business, or maybe a change in corporate strategy.

Management can also come and go from one financial quarter to the next in many organizations. You might have an awesome manager one day who believes in you, gives you a lot of freedom, and regularly recognizes your accomplishments.

Then, bam! That person leaves and gets replaced by someone with a completely different approach. Maybe they micromanage, which you might despise. Or, they might want to do things their way, which happens to be vastly different from the way you operate. They might just see something you don't. The best thing you can do in such a situation is try to work with the new manager as much as possible. If you give it an honest effort and for some reason, you still can't get behind their approach, maybe it's time to look for a new opportunity.

Challenge yourself to embrace change, condition yourself to expect it, and consider it an opportunity. It's not easy, but you'll be much better off if you learn how to deal with change effectively. Others may get so frustrated when organizational plans are altered that they leave the company. That could create an opening for you to add prime territories and have an amazing year. When others surrender, it may be a good idea to keep fighting. Their loss could be your gain.

Game Changer #27: Expect and embrace change by stepping outside of your situation to see the big picture for your company, team, and yourself. Bide your time, keep an open mind, adjust your approach, and course-correct when necessary.

REFRAMING CHANGE AS
PERSONAL CHALLENGE

I remember a conversation with a woman named Alia, who was working in sales for three and a half years for a smaller organization. Her ability to weather the storm related to change was impressive. She had a knack for handling every sort of uncertainty the business world could hit her with, including significant shifts in her territory, compensation structure, and even the requirements of her role. The following is what she had to say about this flexibility and determination she had in her sales skillset.

"Working on a sales team at a young company, I experienced plenty of change. I dealt with two months of faulty leads, steadily increasing goals, compensation structure adjustments, and managerial shifts. While all that was certainly stressful at times, I tried to reframe those changes as personal challenges.

"Perhaps the key moment for me in learning how to adjust to uncertainty and change was when I reached out to another successful rep at the same company. I knew he had worked his way through a lot of change long before I got there. He helped me develop the resolve to power through it while achieving solid results in the process.

"That organization gave me my first opportunity in a sales role, which I greatly coveted because I knew how valuable the ability to sell was and that it would help me in future roles. I also figured that being able to consistently overcome change seemed like it would keep me on my toes and make me a stronger overall salesperson."

CAPPED!

One of the most difficult circumstances for salespeople to resist succumbing to the dark side is getting capped. I fully understand that companies use caps to manage cost of sale and company performance. From a salesperson's perspective, however, a cap can squash motivation and instill a touch of bitterness. This creates a delicate balancing act for companies when considering the use of caps as part of their sales management efforts.

Occasionally, if you have an unusually good year, the company may choose to put a cap on your earnings. To make this challenge more difficult to deal with, a cap could be accompanied by an increased quota, a decreased territory, or both.

If that happens, there's only one word I can say, which is... Congratulations! A cap means you had a year of stellar performance and that's never a bad thing.

Don't waste your time with bitterness toward the company for capping your income. Instead, be aware that the cap validates you as a top performer and it comes with significantly higher than average compensation. Leverage it with your manager in salary and territory negotiations. Use that cap as a bargaining chip to secure additional resources, or a promotion, as it is proof positive that you can get the job done.

EBBS AND FLOWS

Since the dawn of business, every company has gone through ebbs and flows. Few companies continue to trend upward without the occasional nosedive. Even Amazon hit a period where their stock price took a massive downswing shortly after the dot com bubble burst in the early 2000s, and it took several years for the stock price to recover. Individuals go through ebbs and flows in their careers as well, especially salespeople. How you manage your perspective throughout the good times and bad is absolutely critical.

There are going to be times when you're swamped with work. Mistakes can be made, and stress can feel overwhelming when things are moving fast, especially at the end of the quarter or year. If you find yourself committing errors you don't ordinarily make, take it as a signal to buckle down, prioritize, and get back to your routine. Take solace in knowing that being unusually busy usually means you're going to have a great quarter or year. At a bare minimum, you're building your skillset by getting in front of clients on a consistent basis.

Conversely, there are also going to be slow times when you can't help but feel a bit desperate. This period of calm might be caused by closing an abundance of deals all at once. Or perhaps you've just taken over a new territory and it's taking longer than usual to hit your stride. If and when periods of calm emerge, use the time wisely to regroup and recharge.

It's natural to start worrying about your career when business seems slow or you're not closing any deals. You might get concerned for your job security. That's a normal reaction, but as uneasy as facing the dark side is, you need to do whatever you can to take your mind off of it, so you can focus most clearly on making sure the deals start flowing again. Read a book, meet up with friends, go for a run, whatever you need to do to stop obsessing.

TAKING THE BLAME

You can go from hero to zero awfully fast when a deal goes sideways, and fingers point the blame in your direction. Even when it's the delivery team or the technology that falls short of expectations, it's likely that blame will make its way back to sales, and it will likely come in the flavor of, "This was over-sold." Or, "Sales didn't set the proper client expectations."

Sometimes blame belongs with the salesperson and other times it doesn't. If you feel blame is being inappropriately placed on you, it's best to take the high road. That doesn't mean you should accept total responsibility for all the problems, but in most cases, you don't need to point your finger in another person's direction either. Instead, work hard to fix the situation or help the delivery team reset expectations. Then, prepare to accept the glory that comes with going from zero back to hero when it gets resolved.

Implementation and delivery roles can be extremely taxing. Replacing or implementing a complex solution, while ensuring all downstream processes run properly is very difficult to accomplish. Add the responsibility of driving revenues while decreasing costs to the situation, and you have a highly challenging list of priorities. When those processes go awry, the salesperson is often the recipient of the initial blame. It doesn't always seem appropriate or fair, but that's the traditional path for blame to follow in most of those cases.

What can you do about it?

First of all, don't attempt to "pass the buck," because that is never a good look, especially around people with whom you're trying to foster good relationships. Secondly, make sure you're prepared with the full chain of emails outlining client expectations and timelines, as well as any written conversation concerning implementation, transition, and/or delivery teams. That way, when you see the blame heading your way, you can pull up the emails that prove you set expectations appropriately and transferred sufficient account knowledge to the team taking over the business.

I remember a situation not long ago when blame was traveling swiftly in my direction. It was several months after I closed a pilot deal and transitioned the account. The account manager who took over called me and asked if I promised the client a significant percentage increase in incremental growth in an effort to secure the business.

Promising anything over a modest percent in that particular scenario would set the entire effort up for failure. That would be an unrealistic expectation akin to sending the delivery team over Niagara Falls in a barrel. Understandably, the account manager was angered by the alleged promise I made.

Fortunately for my team and me, I kept the emails that reviewed the client's goals and programs in great detail. Moreover, some of those emails outlined the conversations during the sales process that clearly laid out the expectations for return on investment. In fact, one of them clearly stated that zero uplift was promised during the first phase of the pilot. It went on to state that up to a modest uplift could be achieved in the second phase.

Besides the emails that discussed expectations, I also included all the sales materials I gathered, as well as a transition email I drafted for the new team that was taking over the business.

The account manager discussed the situation directly with the client and used the information I gave her as leverage. After seeing the information laid out so thoroughly, the client responded, "I must have confused that percentage lift with a case study I read about somewhere else during my research."

Keep in mind that a modest lift in business may not sound like an enormous win, but when dealing with a mature business that conducts regular transactions in the millions of dollars, even a small increase can be quite significant. In the end, the client was pleased to achieve the results we delivered.

Game Changer #28: Expect delivery shortfalls or missed client expectations to get blamed on sales. Dive deep into your client's expectations during the sales process, clearly document them, and conscientiously transition the deal accordingly.

ACQUISITIONS AND REORGANIZATIONS

Big companies have big appetites and they buy smaller companies all the time. I mentioned previously how Adobe acquires smaller organizations somewhat regularly. That's not uncommon for large companies in today's current business cycle.

Personally, I've been through at least four or five major acquisitions in my career. I've served as a member on several integration teams and helped to scope out targets and run market scans as acquisition precursors. Beyond that, I've also seen the impact these efforts have on organizations and their people many times.

Acquisitions and reorganizations are a "certain uncertainty" in the business world. They're certain to happen, but it's uncertain when and how it will all settle.

When an acquisition happens, it's likely going to entail some changes for your role. You might become part of a new team or report to new people. You may need to develop new areas of domain experience, sell new products or features, or even completely revamp your go-to-market approach.

Reorganization, which will occasionally happen regardless of whether or not an acquisition occurred, can propel you forward or push you down. You'll see people vaulted into positions of power almost overnight, and you'll see people firmly in the grip of the dark side, clinging tenaciously to the way things were while fueling their own demise. Collaborate with the new people who come along, while maintaining existing relationships. Burn no bridges and someday you'll see a crowd of supporters willing to help you in a time of need.

Acquisitions and reorganizations are going to happen many times throughout your career, and there's nothing you can do about it. There's no point in wasting too much of your time worrying and speculating about it. Over time, you'll notice that those who expend their energies in that way either don't stick around or are asked to leave. If you value the vision of your company, focus on helping the team to deliver it. Pour your energy into becoming an example of what your company aspires to be.

> Game Changer #29: While acquisitions and reorganizations can cause periods of uncertainty and disruption, they can also create opportunities to build new skills, develop new relationships, close new types of deals, and fill new roles.

BURNED CLIENTS

No matter how hard you try to show certain clients that you care about their business and will always do what's best for them, some of them are always going to be distrusting of you. Some clients can't shake their fear and mistrust, no matter how hard you try. You could be the most caring, genuine, and talented person in the world, but they won't see anything but a line item expense to squeeze.

When that happens, don't take it personally. They may think that way because they've been burned in the past, perhaps more than once. Or they may pride themselves on getting the best deal possible for their company. That situation most likely has nothing to do with you, so move on when you're involved with a particularly severe version of that demeanor.

If you can't move on, continue to showcase your caring attitude, along with your skillset to deliver value and maybe you'll win them over...eventually. Maybe you won't, but if you're not able to get through to them, chances are you're not alone and they might not be around long. Alternatively, you can go higher in the organization for additional support. More on this in Part IV.

INTERNAL COMPETITION

Occasionally, you might find yourself in a challenging internal environment. Some team members may have a natural inclination to compete, rather than collaborate, even at the expense of the overall team performance. The best thing to do in that situation is to not get dragged down into the mud with people who misdirect their competitive energy within their team and do not have the big picture of the team's success on their agenda.

You could also find yourself in a situation where internal teams have conflicting financial incentives. That can be an especially difficult situation. When that happens, the best approach is to find a win-win, speak frankly, and do what's right for your client, your company, and yourself.

Being known as a team player is a valuable trait to have as part of your reputation. A little internal competition is healthy and fun but not to the point where the team suffers. If you find yourself working with an overly competitive individual, strive to be the top player, but don't be the person that does it by making others look bad or incompetent. Those individuals will be weeded out over time.

 Game Changer #31: If you're in a positive work environment, where you're working with great people, learning a lot, and making good money, savor it!

DON'T TAKE THE DARK SIDE HOME WITH YOU

We're all susceptible to the dark side. When it comes calling, the most important thing to remember is to not bring it home with you. It's beyond easy to get sucked into these challenging circumstances, especially if you're surrounded by others with a negative outlook on the team, the company, or themselves.

Aside from occasionally soliciting advice, don't take those dark moments home with you and let them interfere with your personal life. These days, a lot of couples are made up of two working professionals, and it's more likely than ever before that someone carries some work drama home.

Mismanaging the dark side will not only jeopardize your professional life and work relationships, but if you take that burden home with you, it will also ruin your nights, weekends, vacations, special moments, and just about everything else.

I'm still not immune to the dark side; I wonder if anybody truly is, but I'm much better at handling it all now than I was when I began my career. There are a few things I can recommend that may help you address any encounter with the dark side of sales.

MANAGE EXPECTATIONS

It takes no time at all to manage expectations appropriately, and that is crucial to your ability to handle change. Make a conscious choice to perceive change and uncertainty the right way. Understand that the game of sales isn't all champagne and roses, but with the right outlook, it can still be an extremely rewarding occupation on many levels.

TAKE ACTION

You don't need to be a Jedi Master to face the dark side of sales, but you do need to take action. If you start losing motivation and feel an air of despair, even for just a couple of days, write the issue down and create a list of actions to break the cycle. If that doesn't work, seek an outsider's perspective. The situation may be a lot better or a lot worse than you think. Either way, seek an honest opinion from somebody you trust and respect. Ask them for suggestions on how to address whatever it is that's dragging you down.

 Game Changer #32: During tough times, develop a regular practice of writing down the things for which you are grateful.

CHECK YOURSELF

Around two to three years ago, I began a self-check exercise every time I felt the dark side impacting my career. Once or twice a week, I took less than three minutes when I woke up, and wrote down three things for which I am grateful.

That simple routine has been helpful to a mind-blowing level, because it serves as an excellent reminder that there are many more things to be grateful for than there are things to be worried about. It will help you to most effectively manage times of heightened uncertainty. When you remind yourself of how many good things are around you, the dark side loses some of its grip. Such an activity allows you a much-needed reset when you need it most.

THE FROZEN TUNDRA

We've all had occasional moments of doubt concerning our territory. One of my more memorable and recent encounters with the dark side happened when I first joined Adobe. I worked diligently and patiently with a tough client list. The clients I met with were all smart and well intentioned, but they weren't ready to drive action. You might say they were a bit chilly to the idea of commitment, which is why I dubbed that territory, the frozen tundra.

My solution consultant at the time was a man by the name of Marco Turner. He was unflappable no matter how esoteric or aggressive the line of technical questions from clients or partners. After one especially icy meeting we had with a client, he emerged shaking his head a little and said, "Oomph!" That was pretty rough."

I agreed with his exasperated response and self-consciously asked him, "How is everybody else doing?"

Marco paused for a moment, most likely not wanting to say anything too negative or non-supportive, and said, "Their clients are much easier to deal with."

Earlier in my career I might have decided to leave the company. I'm sure that plenty of salespeople would have done exactly that. Yet, I came to the conclusion that the list of clients was beyond my control, and complaining to management for a new one would not have been well received. At that point, I realized that it was a better idea for me to work hard within the confines of my territory that was in my control. So, I made a special effort to take extra time to brainstorm solutions.

A few weeks later, I started to see the light emerge from the darkness. Ideas began to surface, and I saw a path to bring in a ridiculous amount of revenue. I dedicated significant time for preparation and follow-through.

It seemed like a heat wave of deals to thaw the frozen tundra was in the forecast. I knew I needed to prepare my home life for the expected increase in my time at work. So, I told my wife Arianne all about the situation surrounding the challenging territory I had been assigned. I wanted her to understand if I needed to dedicate extra time to ensuring the solution would click with my client base. She understood and completely supported me.

For the next several months, I put my nose to the grindstone and implemented a systematic approach to thaw the frozen tundra. I had an end goal in mind and faith in my abilities and those of the surrounding team. I never planned on sitting atop the frozen tundra indefinitely.

It was a short-term situation that worked out, because I was able to focus all of my energy on building pipeline. In fact, I was driving toward a tidal wave of deals, which enabled me to become the number one attainment performer in the company a few quarters later. That success would have never been possible if I didn't devise a plan to thaw the frozen tundra.

The key to victory over the dark side is simply not allowing ourselves to get consumed with anxiety related to our struggles with a tough client base or anything else. It's easy to compound problems by saying to yourself, "I got stuck with a difficult territory, I'm giving up, there's no point." Instead, be solution focused and write down your plan. Then, work tirelessly to execute it and you'll be far better off than if you gave up too easily. Anybody can do this. In fact, you can rely on this approach time and time again.

As you prepare to dive into the next chapter about tough conversations, understand that it pertains to some of the most challenging aspects of sales execution that you or anyone else will face.

Change, uncertainty, blame, caps, and other stormtroopers of sales can be challenging adversaries. During the tough times, you'll wish you had a better perspective on how to handle the dark side. Hopefully, this chapter helps you to develop that perspective and power through anything that stands in your way.

I still deal with managing some of the more challenging parts of the dark side, but I'm much better now than I was when I started. I identify issues, take action, and move on much more quickly. If you're struggling with the dark side more often than you'd like, try putting these ideas into practice and soon, the dark side of sales will be nothing more than an occasional annoyance, rather than a Death Star capable of blowing up your world.

CHAPTER 8

INITIATING TOUGH CONVERSATIONS

"Hard things are hard because there are no easy answers or recipes. They are hard because your emotions are at odds with your logic. They are hard because you don't know the answer and you cannot ask for help without showing weakness."

—BEN HOROWITZ (VENTURE CAPITALIST, AUTHOR, FORMER CEO OF OPSWARE)

A few weeks ago, I was in a taxi on my way to a client meeting while listening to an internal deal review call with senior management. These calls are helpful because they discuss deals on many different levels. They provide insight on how sellers are thinking about deals and management's feedback on how to proceed.

While listening to these calls, a common theme emerged... almost all of the cycles involved could have benefited from greater initiative in having the tough conversations with clients necessary to move the deals forward. These themes included delivery problems, misaligned expectations, new client-side senior management directives (also known as, "our priorities have changed"), and others.

With that in mind, you might be wondering what exactly constitutes a tough conversation?

For the purpose of this chapter, a tough conversation is any external discussion related to your deal that might be perceived as difficult and uncomfortable.

Tough conversations can be related to urgent issues like changing expectations, deal opposition, technical issues, and unreasonable demands, or to equally important issues that are non-urgent like complacency. I'll get to the how to have tough conversations soon, but first, I want to discuss some of the reasons you can't avoid them.

THE COST OF AVOIDANCE

It may seem uncomfortable—even unnatural—to steer toward tough conversations, but when circumstances call for it, you're far better off initiating them than avoiding them. It's critical to know what the cost of avoidance is; not just from a financial perspective, but in terms of damaged relationships, reputations, and more. If you don't initiate tough conversations, you risk the following:

- **Reduced deal size**—Bigger deals involve higher stakes. Every large transaction has major hurdles to clear, internally and externally. No matter how good you and your team are, you're going to run into surprises. But if you're not initiating tough conversations, the issues will linger and be more numerous and severe.

- **Lost deals**—Blockers from procurement to legal, security, and others may become insurmountable if you don't initiate the necessary tough conversations. This type of discussion may involve a sit-down with the blockers themselves or a meeting with the client to discuss how to overcome any potential or emerging obstacles.
- **Wasted time**—This can come in many forms, especially concerning the opportunities you choose to focus on the most. By avoiding tough conversations early, you may not gain a true sense for where the client stands. This could result in a time investment into cycles that should have been either approached in a different way or completely abandoned. For example, RFP processes can be time consuming. If you sense a client might be tempted to solicit input from competitors, you need to challenge them with a tough conversation around why an RFP is necessary. If you discover that it can't be avoided, ask to speak with the decision maker in exchange for participating, and help them craft the RFP. If you don't have this tough conversation, you'll likely waste time filling out RFPs that you have slim to no chance of winning. You will get sucked into the column fodder of an RFP that was written for or by your competitors.
- **Lost respect from clients**—If clients don't trust you to challenge them when they could be moving in the wrong direction, they'll be far less likely to value their relationship with you.
- **Team and management concern**—A lack of willingness to own tough conversations will result in lost faith from your team members and management. They need to know you're ready, willing, and able to handle any and all circumstances as they arise.

WHY SALESPEOPLE AVOID TOUGH CONVERSATIONS

If avoiding tough conversations can be so costly in so many ways, you might be wondering why so many salespeople do so. Perhaps we underestimate the negative impact of avoidance. The most common reason for this costly mistake is fear. After that, there may be a knowledge gap involved with identifying when a tough conversation is necessary. Let's start by dissecting how to transform the former and attack the latter.

TRANSFORMING FEAR INTO OPPORTUNITY

Often, we attribute fear as a negative emotion in every way. Fear can be good, however, if it helps you to avoid dangerous situations.

In the business world, you can leverage fear in a positive manner by transforming it from a paralyzing source of inaction to a motivational kickstart that seizes opportunity.

Many salespeople fear tough conversations, because they worry about drawing an adverse response from a client, colleague, or manager. So, they say nothing, and as a result, they get nowhere. Business decisions rooted in fear alone will often lead to poor results and occasionally to disastrous consequences. With that in mind, how do you transform fear into opportunity?

1. Begin your transformation of fear by asking yourself some questions.
    - "What exactly do I fear most in my professional life?"
    - "Is fear holding me back from accomplishing any of my short- or long-term goals?"
    - "How would I solve problems or handle tough conversations if fear wasn't a factor?"

2. Become mindful of the impact fear is having on each situation as it occurs.
3. Take one action that is outside of your comfort zone every day. You could reach out to a key executive, step-up for a high-visibility project, or use a new sales approach. Don't limit your options for transforming fear. Keep an open-mind and try new things.

By following those three steps consistently over a few months, you'll notice a transformation taking place.

- Instead of fearing what others might think, you'll focus on the importance of making your voice heard.
- Instead of fearing conflict, you'll focus on understanding the opposing perspective, which will help you to progress the deal forward by diffusing issues and solving problems.
- Instead of fearing failure, you'll make the decision to consistently give your best effort, realizing that no matter the outcome, you will learn and grow from the experience.

By transforming your fears into opportunities, you'll feel a renewed sense of enthusiasm and excitement about possibilities you would have otherwise missed.

WHEN TO INITIATE TOUGH CONVERSATIONS

Once you're aware of the need to transform fear into opportunity, it will serve you well to know the various circumstances in a sales cycle that can act as triggers for tough conversations. Thinking about these should enable you to anticipate and identify how and when to initiate tough conversations.

You might develop a sixth sense for knowing when something

is off with your client. When you think something might be going sideways in a deal, you'll be ready to take action quickly before it becomes a big problem.

Let's take a look at some of the common triggers you should expect to encounter. The following diagram contains my top five and provides specific examples of each. Notice how they're broken down into two categories because they need to be handled differently.

Triggers for Tough Conversations

URGENT AND IMPORTANT TRIGGERS			
1. Deal Opposition	**2. Changed Expectations**	**3. Unrealistic Demands**	**4. Technical Issues**
When someone close to the deal is overtly resistant to your solution or even actively working against it. This person is a blocker whose concerns need to be acknowledged and addressed sooner rather than later.	When your client's scope of needs changes. This involves reworked contract terms, pricing, and aligned resources if you're far down the path.	When the client, or more often, procurement, doesn't have an accurate understanding of your offer and is making unrealistic demands concerning pricing, resources, information, timelines, or other deal parameters.	When a product or feature used by your client is being phased out. The client won't be happy about this news, but this could provide an opportunity to offer an alternative solution that the client may appreciate even more.
NON-URGENT TRIGGERS			
5. Complacency When the client is convinced that doing nothing is the best path because they don't see a need for your offer, or they don't recognize there is even a problem to resolve in the first place.			

Another important thing to keep in mind is that all these types of external conversations serve as indicators that you may not be getting aligned properly with your client's senior management. Top executives have the authority and the ability to make all the issues behind these interactions go away...most of the time.

You will, however, encounter some situations where a tough conversation is unavoidable, regardless of how much support the deal has from the highest levels of the organization.

HOW TO INITIATE *URGENT* TOUGH CONVERSATIONS

Do your analysis before the conversation and make sure you have a full understanding of what everybody's goals are. If you're engaged in a tough conversation about a challenging technical issue between your product and the customer's environment, get a grasp of how to fix the issue, and work with your client towards the optimal solution as proactively as you can. Whatever the situation is, the tough conversation is your chance to turn it around.

Once you're thoroughly prepared, I suggest following a simple, three-step process for engaging in tough conversations. This process enables you to express empathy because you'll be identifying with the situation and confirming it with the other party. By following this process, you'll demonstrate a willingness to partner on a mutually agreeable solution, rather than acting as an adversary getting ready for confrontation.

The beauty is in how it enables you to be assertive, not aggressive, which are two distinctly different states. I've used it myself and seen it used effectively by others countless times.

The conversation likely won't be easy. These simple steps will, however, help you to move towards some type of thoughtful resolution, whatever that might be.

1. **Confirm the situation**—Confirm you have an accurate understanding of what needs to be addressed by describing your assessment of the situation in detail to the other party.

2. **Explore options**—Solicit ideas from the other party and discuss various possibilities for a solution that satisfies everyone's best interests. If there is only one solution, make it clear why that is the case, and fully explain the downside if no action is taken,

3. **Define actions**—Once you've both agreed to a viable alternative, develop a plan of action, a timeline, and assign clear ownership of each task to the appropriate individual.

Structuring your conversation in this manner will make it a much less daunting task. Not all tough conversations will have a happy ending, but everyone will remember the effort you put forth in managing the situation and your collaborative approach to finding a solution. That act alone could provide great dividends for you in the future with amicable long-term relationships.

THE HEAT IS ON: THE THREE STEPS IN ACTION

If you think sales is high-pressure with a lot of heat, you're correct. But while salespeople put our mittens in the oven to pull out a deal now and then, Proof of Concept (PoC) teams live in the oven.

PoC teams manage several intense engagements at the same time, each of which might have a strategic multi-million-dollar deal hinging upon its success. They have to do it all while new technology is being implemented, new processes are designed, existing processes are being modified, and new talent is being introduced.

Every meeting POC teams have can involve at least one tough conversation, where they could be addressing changed expectations, fixing critical technology issues, and facing unrealistic demands at the same time.

Here's what a POC leader I've worked with in the past had to say about her tough conversations:

"We won't consider moving forward unless there are clear expectations set with the client. Those conversations are never as simplistic as you might expect. So, we kick the tires in a few different ways to make sure everyone involved understands what success will look like. It's documented down to specific metrics, and we're always sure to provide options for how we might proceed."

In a nutshell, they confirm the situation, explore options, and define plans of action. If it works for them, this approach will work for you as well.

BUILD INTERNAL SUPPORT

There will be many points throughout your career when it's all on the line—the make or break moments. This could involve a meeting with a senior executive regarding a deal-breaking issue that needs to be fixed. Sometimes, an entire client relationship hangs in the balance of one conversation. It's definitely all on the line in those situations.

Ensure you have the necessary internal executive buy-in to support the alternative solutions you design. Senior management may have the ability to create special terms for pricing, services, or other parameters that you don't have the authority to approve. This is powerful support that can come in handy when a deal is about to either close or vanish like perfume in the wind.

Notify your management team of the risks involved before a tough conversation takes place, especially if you anticipate that a deal or even an existing client relationship is at stake. You can't be afraid to highlight the issue in this situation, because if the engagement with the client—new or existing—continues to decline, your management team can provide insight on your proposed alternatives, prioritize them, strengthen them, contribute new recommendations, and perhaps even save the relationship.

ALL HANDS ON DECK

I recall one particularly serious situation I was involved with where getting management's support was critical to saving an extremely valuable opportunity.

We were far along in the sales cycle when the situation began to unfold. I received an email from my customer success manager, who was on the ground overseeing the day-to-day account activity. He told me that our consulting team had just had such a horrible meeting that the whole deal was about to disintegrate, and so was all of the existing business with that client as well.

Our consulting team had already met with the client countless times before, but a new consulting team member had been added to the meeting, and for whatever reason, that person just didn't click with the client. To make matters worse, a brand-new client-side senior executive, whom we never met with before, made a last-minute surprise appearance. He wanted to discuss concrete recommendations for a twenty-four-month roadmap, which he thought should have been prepared months ago. Unfortunately, our consulting team wasn't ready to discuss that yet.

The disconnect was due to poor preparation, unfamiliarity of a new team member, misaligned expectations, etc. Whatever the case was, the meeting went so poorly, the new executive not only wanted to blow up the deal but also said he was strongly considering going to RFP on all our technologies installed. (Now might be a good time to revisit the chapter on horrible meetings.)

It might seem natural to try to take on the responsibility for fixing that situation on your own. This could be out of supreme but misplaced confidence, fear of senior managers placing the blame on you for the issue even occurring in the first place, or perhaps you really can fix it.

A problem this urgent and potentially fatal to the overall

client relationship, however, should not be handled by one person or kept under wraps. This is a classic case of when to get *all-hands-on-deck* and notify all the people who can make a difference.

The second I saw that email, I alerted senior management to get them onboard with my suggestions for remedying the situation. I brought the issue to the attention of managers and executives up and down the organizational food chain. The goal was to solicit high-level feedback, cover all the angles, and prevent surprises from happening. I wanted to rally as much support as possible to salvage the deal and the relationship.

We also brought together a few teams from different departments to collaborate on our plan to turn the situation around. Ultimately, we swapped out the person on the implementation team who wasn't a good fit onto another project. We also presented a parallel recommendation in case the client changed their minds about our original solution.

Soon enough, our senior executives reached out to the client's leadership team, and all of these actions combined to form a broad-based partnership, internally and externally, that would fully support the proposed solution and close the deal.

Our quick and efficient actions demonstrated how capable our team was to bounce back from adversity, which gave the client the confidence they needed to proceed.

Within a week or two, we had meetings scheduled on-site to get things back on track. That would have never been possible if I hadn't sprinted towards preparing my team for the tough conversation and notified all the appropriate parties within minutes of getting that initial panic-inducing email. Time was of the essence and sitting on that email for even a couple days could have had a drastically negative effect on saving the client relationship, much less getting the deal done.

That example proves how some client relationships may require several tough conversations—both internal and external—to resolve problems and close the deal. It explains the comprehensive benefit of steering towards tough conversations, rather than shying away from them.

Game Changer #35: Interactions that make you feel the most uncomfortable can have the biggest impact. Run towards them.

OVERCOMING CLIENT COMPLACENCY

Having a solid understanding for how to identify urgent tough conversations will be a big boost to your sales skillset. With those tools firmly in place, you will always be prepared for when the need for one may surface. Some tough conversations you can see coming from a mile away.

Other tough conversations lay behind the scenes waiting for just the right moment to appear. Preparation and determination to do what's needed for the deal will be key to executing those successfully. Expected or not, you should be ready to engage in any type of tough conversation, even early in the sales cycle, if necessary.

Sometimes, challenging clients as soon as your introductory

meeting can be exactly what's needed to get the ball rolling for a great deal on the horizon. It doesn't do any good to just sit in their office and tell them everything they want to hear in those early interactions, because you're not really driving any sort of value that way.

CHALLENGING CLIENTS EARLY IN THE SALES CYCLE

If the only thing a client does during your meeting is politely nod their head up and down while saying, "Yes," you should rethink your approach. Don't mistake a lack of pushback in your initial client interactions for an earnest desire to move forward.

This is a classic case of what it can be like to interact with a client who has a lot of complacency behind them. If you're not telling them anything new, they will not see a need to change their current situation. Inaction will seem to be the best option to them. Your job—at that point—is to change their minds.

In my experience, that type of placid yes response doesn't typically lead to a deal. In the client's mind, the only thing you've accomplished is joining the faceless herd of less than extraordinary and unmemorable salespeople they've spoken with... once.

Relax, because we've all been there and done that. Early in our careers, we walk into a client meeting when the client agrees with everything we say, and think to ourselves, "Wow, I killed it in there! They agreed with everything I said."

Then, we follow up with one unreturned phone call and email after another, only to find out that the client wasn't really interested in anything we presented because it wasn't anything new.

In contrast, if you walk into a client meeting and start talking about something completely unexpected, even if it creates a little tension in the room, the customer might perk up soon after and react with, "Whoa! I never thought of that before." At that point, you will have started a dialogue, rather than a standard exchange of routine information and an involuntary muscular reaction of affirmation. In this scenario, you've separated yourself from the faceless herd. Instead, you've become a credible, outside-the-box thinker with unique value. You've become extraordinary.

You should also extend the concept of caring from chapter 3 to the idea of challenging clients, because if you truly care about them, you won't just roll over and let them dictate the entire process.

Tough love is necessary at times. Occasionally, you may have to do something that a team member, third party, or even client may not like very much. You need to prove that you're willing to do what is difficult, unpopular, or both in the short-term to strive for the long-term best interests of all parties.

It might seem counterintuitive to challenge a client during one of your first interactions, but that's okay because most of us feel that way at first. Do whatever you can to overcome that initial discomfort and you'll soon see the results. Remember to listen, be assertive and diplomatic, not aggressive.

Don't just take my word for it. Matthew Dixon and Brent Adamson wrote a book in 2011 called *The Challenger Sale*. The book is based on a Corporate Executive Board study of

6,000 salespeople. It's worth a read if you're looking for an edge on helping companies overcome complacency. In their book, Dixon and Adamson posited that salespeople fall into five major behavioral clusters:

1. The Lone Wolf
2. The Relationship Seller
3. The Reactive Problem Solver
4. The Hard Worker
5. The Challenger

The major discovery this study unlocked was that the "challenger" type of salesperson mopped the floor with everybody else. Challengers especially dominated the arena of complex sales. More than just spitting out some arbitrary sales data, *The Challenger Sale* provides qualitative and quantitative evidence about how and why challengers are so successful.

Recommended Resource: *The Challenger Sale* by Matthew Dixon and Brent Adamson.

For proper perspective, I'd like to clarify what it means to be a *challenger* in the game of sales. It doesn't mean walking into a client's office and immediately throwing down the gauntlet. There's no need to have an arm-wrestling match or any other form of false bravado or pointless confrontation. Establishing some sort of dominance or backing a client into a corner is not the goal. In fact, such an approach would likely result in alienating or offending the client to such a degree, they'll never agree to meet with you again.

The term *challenger* in the context of a salesperson relates to someone who doesn't just walk into an initial client meeting with a generic presentation. Rather, the challenger attempts to educate clients right off the bat, with an industry-based point of view, focused on the unique benefits their company can deliver. This helps clients to see the associated risks with complacency.

EDUCATING CLIENTS ABOUT THEIR PROBLEMS

Every organization has problems, and they likely share common problems with other organizations in their industry. This could be in the form of wasted operating investments, procedural inefficiencies, or a bundle of other problems that induce headaches for your clients. It's never a good idea to attack that pain point as if you were pouring salt on an open wound. Instead, ask questions to validate whatever problems you suspect they might be experiencing. It could be as simple as asking them, "What would you change about that situation if you could?" That's a great way to segue into a discussion of a known problem, as well as uncover some other areas of concern that were previously unknown.

Educating a client about an unknown problem can be difficult. It can also be exciting, however, because it provides a way to reframe their perspective on their entire business, which can go a long way in awakening them to the high value of your input.

There are many ways to educate your clients. One way is to tell them an insightful story around a new economic reality that's been created from the evolving technological landscape. I've seen the following narrative in many forms over the years. It is a great example of educating while challenging your client to think differently:

> "Think about how drastically advertising has changed over the last two decades. As recently as the late 1990s, it consisted almost exclusively of television commercials, print, and billboards. Today's media consumer, however, has a wide array of different channels where your audience can access content—YouTube, Netflix, Hulu, Amazon Prime Video, and many more options—all of which provide advertising options. This proliferation of options has resulted in massive audience fragmentation. Now, I realize that none of that is surprising to anyone who has been awake for the last ten to fifteen years. What is unique, however, is the way my company can address this issue to create new opportunity for your business."

By the end of this type of conversation, you will likely have educated the client on a hidden problem. It could be that for many years, they've incurred unnecessary expenses due to a lack of insight into actual cost and performance from marketing options that have passed their prime, and this has a trickle-down effect that causes a slower time to market, and even misalignment between their strategy and ability to execute.

What this all means for you and me is that a lot of clients work through a bewildering array of inefficient services and ineffective technologies weighing down their operations. Those situations can make it nearly impossible for them to integrate technologies they already own. This means they might not be able to do things like manage how their customers interact with their brand online across different channels.

In severe cases, ongoing operations can become unmanageably expensive to maintain due to an abundance of external service providers that end up preventing the company's employees from taking ownership of their systems, data flows, and ability to directly execute on their overarching business goals.

When drawn on a white board or presented on a PowerPoint, this can cause a client's operations and technology stack to resemble a plate of homemade spaghetti. Sure, fresh spaghetti is delicious, but nobody wants it to be an accurate depiction of their operations.

This is just one example of how an educational approach can disarm while uncovering significant problems. Help your clients gain clarity on their situation and show them why they should take action and how you can help them do it successfully.

Game Changer #36: Clients are always looking for new insights that inspire them. If you can deliver insights that align to your product, your clients will take action.

HANDLE WITH CARE

Questioning the effectiveness of your client's existing partnerships and technology decisions is going to be a tough conversation. It's going to get even tougher when you challenge their ability to drive results based on those potential shortcomings. Yet, it's the best way to raise a client's awareness of the severity of those problems and how significant value can be created for their company (and yours) by fixing them.

These types of conversations need to be handled with great care, because they can force companies to completely re-evaluate their strategy, which can cause volatile reactions. Therefore, it's natural for a salesperson to fear having them, but big deals can be lost or never attempted if you shy away from such an interaction. Over time, engaging in tough conversations will become second nature. You might even start to like them because you know you're at the cusp of driving positive change for your clients.

Game Changer #37: Average salespeople sell products. Great salespeople reframe and educate to challenge their client's perspective, and they do it with credibility that leads to positive change.

By initiating tough conversations early in the client relationship, and being prepared to face them throughout the sales cycle, you're paving the way for a smoother process. The client knows right away that you're not afraid to tackle tough issues. Keep that thought fresh in your mind as you approach the next chapter, which is about risk. It's also wise to anticipate and even attack risk early in your sales cycles. Read on to find out why.

Game Changer #38: You'll know you've mastered initiating tough conversations when you routinely convert them into moments of deal progression, expansion, and creation.

PART 4

PEAK PERFORMANCE

CHAPTER 9

DON'T JUST MANAGE RISK, ATTACK IT!

"There are risks and costs to action. But they are far less than the long-range risks of comfortable inaction."

—JOHN F. KENNEDY (THIRTY-FIFTH PRESIDENT OF THE UNITED STATES)

Mastering risk is essential to taking your sales career to the next level, which is why I recommend tackling it head on rather than taking a passive approach, as if it might go away by ignoring it. Many times, the only thing standing between you and closing a big deal is some form of risk, so you'll want to devote serious time to learning all about it.

So much of what we've covered to this point is about risk. Value selling, project management, initiating tough conversations, learning from horrible meetings—they're all general sales practices to attack risk, directly or indirectly.

In a perfect world, any form of risk would be immediately identified by a giant electronic billboard flashing "RISK" in brilliant neon red. Whereas some of the risks we've already talked about aren't quite that easy to identify, you can still see them coming from far enough away to react before they become a problem. Other forms of risk, however, aren't so easy to spot. There is no neon lettering to read in those cases. Usually, the only time you recognize those forms of risk is when the client has every reason in the world to buy... but doesn't, and you didn't see it coming. You should be hunting for risk at the beginning of your client interactions and throughout the sales cycle. By proactively looking for all the things that can go wrong, you'll be ready for anything that could otherwise severely delay the closing or obliterate the deal altogether. Don't just manage risk, attack it!

 Game Changer #39: Attack risk early and throughout the sales cycle. Become familiar with all the ways your deal can get derailed, so you can anticipate and adjust accordingly.

 Game Changer #40: Put yourself in your client's shoes, and make sure to understand and eliminate all the reasons why they might not be able to sign.

HAPPY EARS

When you have a meeting like the one I mentioned in chapter 8 (Initiating Tough Conversations), when the client politely nods their head up and down, while saying, "Yes," and "Okay," and "Sounds great," throughout the meeting, you might be falling victim to a condition I like to call happy ears. That's when you hear everything you want to hear, encounter zero resistance, and your expectations fly through the roof.

Happy ears is a condition that allows risk to creep into a deal and can cause salespeople to think their deals are larger and more of a sure thing than they actually are. Fortunately, there's a simple antidote. You just need to understand precisely why the client won't buy.

It might be comforting to know that nobody is immune to Happy Ears. Everybody, at some point in their career, has become swept up in a wave of misinterpreted signals and been crushed when a deal failed to come to fruition.

Happy Ears happens to all of us. One of the most common results is we end up accelerating the sales process too quickly after an outstanding meeting, and ignore some key tactical steps that we should have investigated further, either with the client or within our company. For instance, you might be asking procurement to operate a sequence of events that aren't possible within the timeline you need. You could also be forgetting to vet key legal parameters (indemnity, liability, privacy, etc.). What if there are terms in your agreement the client's legal team isn't likely to agree to?

All those scenarios represent risk that could delay or kill a deal it if it occurs unexpectedly toward the end of a closing. However, if you anticipate these risks early in the sales cycle, you'll be ready to handle them without any real damage to the deal itself or the long-term client relationship.

Game Changer #41: What you don't know about the deal can kill it. Don't let Happy Ears stop you from identifying risks early and attacking them before they derail the whole process.

ANTICIPATING BLOCKERS

If you're attacking risk correctly, you may get accused of being somewhat paranoid. That's okay, because what some people interpret as a form of neurosis, more experienced sales leaders will see as due diligence.

I recommend periodically holding meetings with an agenda centered specifically on attacking risk, especially down the stretch with your core team. Ask each team member which issues they think have the biggest potential for becoming a deal blocker. Often times, someone will come up with a potential problem that you nor anyone else had thought of, which could not have been solved without sufficient lead time. This allows you and your team to work systematically towards solutions that eliminate risk as you encounter them.

Game Changer #42: Make it a habit to brainstorm with your team what the risks are and how you will overcome them.

Sales veterans will recognize and appreciate the ways you attempt to anticipate blockers and are prepared to overcome them when necessary. If you're relatively new to the game of sales and not sure what types of things you should be looking for to go wrong, take a look at the following sample list of potential barriers:

- Technical implementation challenges.
- Changes in client-side technical policies.
- New or evolved industry regulations.
- Major new releases from your competitors.
- Legal gridlock.
- Unexpected Service Level Agreement (SLA) demands.
- Statement of Work (SOW) triggering a second procurement cycle. (Different support teams at your client are pulled in review SOWs vs. technology agreements, possibly attached to different budgets).
- Unexpected layers to security reviews.
- Credit Risk and/or Billing Block: Poor bill payment history or outstanding invoices on the part of your client leads your finance team to block the deal.
- Personal health issues on either side of the deal.
- Lack of executive alignment on either side of the deal. (This one is particularly complex to tackle, so review the "power" section of the ValueSelling® framework in chapter 5 and especially the next chapter on deal team.)
- Personnel change. The client hires a decision maker who happens to be from your competitor.
- Alternative vendors get alerted to your opportunity.
- Unforeseen gaps in project management.
- Lack of support from procurement (e.g. they initiate an extended RFP process to further "test the market" as part of your cycle).

That's just a small list to get you started in your approach for anticipating and attacking risk. There's a lot more that can challenge you... *a lot more.* With that in mind, be vigilant, and strive to anticipate and mitigate risk whenever possible.

 Game Changer #43: Create a complete list of risks associated with your specific product or solution to capture the vast majority of potential deal killers.

A PROBLEMATIC PIXEL

While working at Google, I learned one of my hardest lessons on managing risk. It seemed like we had everything lined up perfectly to close a new revenue stream with a large client in the software industry.

The client's VP of marketing was emphatically onboard, which on the surface made the deal appear as close to done as can be, without the signed paperwork. Their agency was also playing along quite nicely, until... here comes the learning opportunity.

As I talked about on a couple of occasions, just because everybody was yessing us to death doesn't mean there wasn't a problem.

Sometime not too far from when the deal was scheduled to close, about thirty of us were engaged in a meeting. There were around ten team members from the client's side, five or six from Google, and another ten to fifteen people from the client's agency. We were all seated at a large oval table with floor-to-ceiling windows around the room, overlooking a beautiful tree-lined street in NYC. The purpose of the meeting was to bring all the stakeholders together and talk about the overall relationship and new opportunities.

Our agenda was moving along nicely, when a problem surfaced...rather loudly.

There had been an ongoing issue with something called the Google Display Pixel, which was a crucial element for us to track conversions in our display campaigns and leverage signals for retargeting.

WHAT IS A PIXEL?

In case you're wondering, a pixel is a piece of code that can be embedded into a website, banner, or email to track visits, digital ad impressions, conversions, or some other type of data related to user activity. It's a critical piece of code to track display media campaigns.

It was also an incredibly easy thing for a company to do. Usually, even big companies can place a pixel on their website within a day. So, even though it sounds incredibly trivial, it was kind of a big deal for our side, because a multi-million-dollar revenue stream was in the balance.

The issue that had droned on for years finally hit the point of no return. Fed up with the lack of progress and exasperated at discussing the situation yet again, our client's VP suddenly slammed his hands on the table, and bellowed, "This is the third year in a row we're talking about this! Get this pixel on our site now!"

There may have even been an expletive or two thrown into

that abrupt demand; I can't say for sure. Either way, you could have heard a pin drop at that moment. Anytime a businessperson raises their voice to a socially uncomfortable volume and accentuates it with a hard slam of the table, awkwardness takes over the room. The outburst was especially impactful given how poised the VP normally was during these meetings.

Remaining seated and resisting the temptation to respond with any sort of equivalent drama, someone from the agency calmly and coolly replied, "We will turn around a point of view on that within sixty days."

Suddenly, awkwardness was replaced with a strange combination of dread and humor, as I detected a slight aspect of enjoyment from the agency in their response, knowing that there was no way in hell they were going to put that pixel on the site. Smartly, they also realized that the VP would assuredly get sidetracked with one of the million other things on his executive to-do-list from managing and growing billions of dollars in revenue across his Americas business and forget all about the pixel problem.

In this case, the agency owned the pixel deployment, which enabled them to stonewall us completely. Worse still, the impact to the client was that it prevented them from increasing lead efficiency and lead volume.

Did my team and I have Happy Ears in the meetings that led to that outcome?

Probably.

Did we attack risk hard enough in the beginning of the client and vendor interactions?

Probably not.

Was I sufficiently focused on searching for blockers in that deal and working on overcoming them?

Definitely not.

In reality, I should have put a lot more work into getting the technical aspect of that deal primed for success. Instead, I let myself get yessed to death by the agency. I didn't kick the tires enough to actually get the pixel on the site.

As a result, the project management dimension of that deal was overlooked. I missed it completely, because I overestimated the client's ability to get their agency to move. The whole situation proved embarrassing because I failed to identify a form of risk that should have been addressed much earlier in the sales cycle.

In hindsight—which is always 20/20—if I would have spoken with the client's VP much earlier about the pixel, I almost certainly would have realized that the issue had been lingering from previous years. Likewise, if I probed the agency harder about the situation before that meeting, I would have had a full picture of why they might not place the pixel on the site.

With a little more preparedness, I might have at least been able to prepare the VP for the agency's response (or lack thereof), and discuss how to address the situation. In that case, he may have simply asked the agency, "What exactly is involved with getting the pixel on the site? Does it take a day, two days, a week...? Please have it done by the end of the week and we're all set."

Rather than adopting the wait-and-see approach, you want to be proactive in seeking blockers that can impede your deal progress. Be laser-focused on risk, because it will create streamlined interactions and processes, while minimizing reactive, last-minute scrambling. Ultimately, your deals will be smoother, with less unnecessary tension. Sales doesn't need to be stressful or laden with drama. By being prepared with all the potential risks of all your deals, the game of sales can be fun and played well enough to win.

Game Changer #44: While focusing on risk, be careful not to zero in on a specific teammate, partner, or team. Instead of casting blame and creating tension, focus on the actions that need to be taken to bring the deal home

Game Changer #45: While brainstorming what might go wrong, never lose your optimism and excitement for how you can help your client succeed.

Attacking risk is critical to managing the sales cycle effectively. For future reference, that's *attack risk* and *manage the sales cycle,* not the other way around. Essentially, it all comes down to being supremely prepared for every situation in every deal.

The next chapter discusses another critical aspect of that

preparation, which is optimizing the strengths of all stake-holders. Often, assembling a dream team that complements each other's skills and works cohesively throughout the sales cycle proves to be the difference maker in a deal getting done.

CHAPTER 10

ASSEMBLING THE DREAM TEAM

"Great things in business are never done by one person; they're done by a team of people."

—STEVE JOBS (AMERICAN BUSINESS ICON)

Deals are rarely closed by one person. A carefully orchestrated team effort, made up of individuals with various special skills and expertise, is required to close a deal. I've always understood that to some extent, but I do remember a moment in my career when that sentiment rang especially true.

I was sitting in my office, trying to refocus my energies on the next opportunity, when I received an email from the leader of the pilot team that helped close my most recent deal. It was the largest one across the team for that quarter and a big win, because it included the entire product line from our business unit, support services, and an embedded partner. The email subject succinctly said, "Time to ring the bell!"

In the enterprise sales world, "ring the bell" means it's time to let the broader team know that a big deal just got closed. Furthermore, it tells everyone to take a victory lap and get ready to do it again, because another big deal is always on the way.

My primary goal was to make sure everybody received the proper shout-out for their contribution to the win. As the lead on that particular deal, I was responsible for sending the email.

As I started writing, the names of various people started coming to me. The deal was about a year and a half in the making, so several departments and multiple levels of management were involved. I stopped writing when I arrived at sixty names on my list.

Game Changer #46: Assemble your deal team expansively across departments, levels of management, and external parties.

After a lot of internal debate, I chopped the list down to thirty, but that hardly seemed fair. It was a humbling process and a bit surprising to realize how many people played a role in winning the business. There were thirty people who made critical contributions for that deal. Without them, I don't think closing it would have been possible.

Some conflicting thoughts came over me. I was delighted that I was surrounded by so many skilled professionals, and that we got to share in a big team win. But I also started to wonder if my involvement in that deal was really as critical as I initially thought it was.

I finished writing the email, and as I pressed the send button, I became awestruck by how everyone pulled together to provide their unique expertise and insight. In the end, it didn't matter who contributed what. What meant the most was that the team supported each other and had direct impact on individual successes across the board.

The rest of this chapter is devoted to describing—in detail—the significant impact that team members and other stakeholders can have on the outcome of a deal, as well as different tactics you can implement to fully assemble the unique qualities needed from various points of the organization to close each individual deal.

DEFINING YOUR APPROACH

The people I mention in this section personify what it means to be great at assembling a dream team. What's interesting is that they use three completely different approaches to drive outstanding results, proving that many paths to success exist in the game of sales.

Hopefully, by learning a little about how these people operate, you'll be able to pick and choose certain qualities and skills that can help you to establish your own approach to assembling a dream team.

The first person that comes to mind when I think of sales role models is Steve Fay. He has such deep knowledge of Adobe's products that he could easily transition to any role on any deal team. He could take on a job in management, as a specialist, or act as technical consultant, and would be equally great at all of them.

He's developed an ability to precisely inform the client how Adobe's products would integrate with their existing systems and processes. Steve has in-depth technological experience that adds supreme value to any client with which he collaborates.

His ability to investigate how his clients have deployed their technology to come up with an accurate assessment of an optimized implementation path is legendary. His vision for how to enhance their overall marketing and advertising operations with our products and services at a granular and strategic level is just as impressive.

Beyond that, Steve's verbal delivery of such results is as well thought out as a comprehensive McKinsey style consultation. The biggest difference is that Steve accomplishes the task in about one-tenth of the time.

Michael Lacy always pinpoints exactly what the ideal path needs to be to get the deal done as quickly as possible, and in the way that provides the best results for all parties. He does this by getting to know his clients at each level in the hierarchy, including the C-Suite. That enables him to most accurately interpret the correct business problems and offer solutions that address the needs of the organization holistically.

Perhaps most importantly, Michael places great emphasis on developing and nurturing client partnerships through the strength of his extended team. His signature strategy is to level-up the scale of relationships for each team member. In other words, if you're working with a manager at a client's organization, Michael gets you aligned with the director. If you're already dealing with the director, he gets you access to the VP, and so on.

Bill Sellers is another prime example of what a great team leader looks like. He places an emphasis on trusting the team to get the job done. At the same time, he knows when to check in at critical junctures to offer help when needed.

His forte is in finding the various strengths within his team, putting faith in them, and ensuring they have all the same deep client knowledge that he has. Listening to his account review is like getting plugged into the Matrix. Even for new team members, his synopsis makes them feel like they've been aligned with the account for many years. He also has an incredible knack for rallying the right resources to overcome seemingly intractable client impasses or internal blockers.

Game Changer #47: Adopt the behaviors and tactics of those you admire and make them your own. There are many paths to strong leadership, and this will help you find your path.

The importance of team leadership becomes especially clear when you realize how it forms and shapes your immediate team. You can control some things in the sales cycle, but others you have no power to manage.

Team assembly is likely one aspect you do not have complete control over. It's still your responsibility, however, to bring everyone on the team up to speed. It's not good enough to simply take care of your own to-do-list and stand by as others struggle or the team fails to meet its objectives.

Your own management style, how you interact with other team members, and how you contribute to the overall team performance are always firmly within your control, and they all contribute significantly to the efficiency and overall results of a deal.

ADDRESSING TEAM STRENGTHS AND WEAKNESSES

Another thing beyond your control is the various strengths and weaknesses that exist throughout your team. That's not such a bad thing, however. The key to success is to work well within that understanding. Expose the strengths and limit or eliminate the weaknesses.

Each team member will have certain areas of high skill, as well as areas of vulnerability. Find a way to enable everybody to succeed by assigning them tasks and ownership of areas that leverage their unique strengths. Meanwhile, address whatever areas of weakness they have by providing proper assistance or eliminating those aspects from a person's responsibilities when possible.

Working within the strengths and weaknesses of a team creates an air of comfort and security, which will prove highly valuable and pay dividends in results from a consistently positive team morale.

Some team members could be new to the organization and not familiar with how to handle key aspects of their role on the team. If that's the situation, you need to connect with that person to let them know you're seeking additional assistance, so they can learn along the way. This way, you reduce the risk of that individual harming the deal.

> Game Changer #48: Carefully consider each individual's role on the team. Understand their specific strengths and weaknesses. Fill gaps where needed and position them for success.

You'll also need to have an accurate view of your own weaknesses, because you'll need to find people on your team who have the skills you lack to fill those gaps as well. If you've never come to terms with your weaknesses before, it's not hard. All you need to do is listen. Your colleagues and clients will let you know if there's anything you're lacking in your interactions with them.

> Game Changer #49: Always keep an open mind to feedback from clients and colleagues.

> Game Changer #50: Rely on your individual strengths as a team leader and find others you can trust to cover your weaknesses with their strengths.

MVP INTERNAL CONTACTS

Cross-departmental contacts, however, are well within your power to establish. Getting to know them can pay enormously high dividends for you, especially when their input/expertise could be the determining factor in whether or not a deal gets done.

Ideally, you want to assemble as many solid contacts within the organization as soon as you possibly can. In a way, this is another form of time savings. For example, by knowing who to go to—right away—in the legal department, you'll be much more likely to get the answers you need in a timely manner for a make-or-break contract clause with a client.

It helps to be tightly aligned with strong players throughout the organization you're working for. A good contact in the legal department is just one example of how valuable it is to assemble your dream team. Other key contacts include team members with product, technical, and services expertise. Valuable players can also come from deal support, top-tier executives, business development, and from your client. Realistically, it helps to have good people in every organizational specialty. I'll discuss how each of these areas can add value to your team.

Game Changer #51: Meeting key people in each department is a great way to establish internal relationships across the business for when you need critical help during the deal cycle. Build those interdepartmental relationships right away. Don't wait until the deal calls for it, because by then, it might be too late.

PRODUCT AND TECHNICAL EXPERTISE

Proving your team understands the match between the technology you're selling and the client's environment is one of the fastest ways to achieve credibility with the folks who manage day-to-day operations. At times, I've been tempted to take shortcuts and assume things will work out. I've learned, however, that's not a good idea.

That sort of short-sightedness has left me especially vulnerable to wasting everyone's time in the long-run. On occasion, the lack of preparation resulted in the oversight of an issue that surfaced later to derail the deal.

Sometimes, I was able to patch things together anyway, but only after a lot of unnecessary grief and stress. Whereas, if I would have just taken a few weeks of lead time to attack that risk instead of exposing myself to it, I could have addressed the issue before it even became a problem.

Having a specialist or solution consultant on the team who can go deep on the technology you are selling is key. They'll be able to help you anticipate the various technical risks. Technical subject matter experts will also make sure you have the correct documentation as reference for your client. These dream team members will run software demos and align company solutions with the client's needs. Having product and technical expertise on your dream team is an invaluable asset, because it ensures your recommendations are sound and you're not unknowingly overpromising anything. If you have any authority to pick one team member, this is probably a good place to use that power.

INDUSTRY MARKETING AND SUBJECT MATTER EXPERTS

If you're working for a large company, you probably have an abundance of internal resources at your disposal. The company may have specific presentations you can use to guide your own interactions. Better than that, you likely have an abundance of internal experts available to handle some of the more esoteric topics involved with unique clients.

For example, Adobe had something called "core services." It

was not a revenue generating offering. But it was of special importance to getting full value out of installed technology, because "core services" provided the connective tissue across many Adobe products by offering value-added integrations.

On occasion, subject matter experts with deep knowledge around analytics, audience management, machine learning, etc., can be called upon for input. They provide rich knowledge that demonstrates the depth of a company's bench to the customer. Subject matter experts also offer a unique perspective to evaluating risk and sources of potential value, because they might be able to advise on nuanced ways to leverage the technology and/or integrate applications of which you may not have otherwise been aware.

DEAL SUPPORT

Sales operations, the deal desk, contract support, legal, and account management are a few of the internal departments that can be immeasurably valuable to supporting your deal. They should be considered integral parts of your dream team. It's crucial to achieve buy-in from them as early in the process as possible.

Personally, I've received some of the best ideas on deal structure and terms from the deal desk and legal departments. Those individuals see an abundance of different commercial offerings that gives them great insight into what is commercially achievable (i.e. what you can get approved internally and what will be approved by the client's legal and procurement teams) to match the needs of various clients, while maximizing bookable revenue. Work on building relationships with these departments, because they have excellent experience in understanding deal structure and how to meet the requirements of all parties involved.

Account management has many years of hands-on experience with your company's products and those of your clients. They've seen it all and can provide a particularly valuable form of expertise, because they manage the day-to-day relationships. Account management can offer specific scenarios to serve as helpful precedent for your clients. If you bring a top account manager into the sales process, they will provide a good example of the type of person your client will be working with to help them manage the business.

An early introduction to this sort of relationship can give your client meaningful peace of mind, knowing more precisely how their ongoing engagement with your company will be handled.

EXECUTIVE BUY-IN

If you're working at a large company, you already know and work with executives who are responsible for hundreds of millions of dollars in revenue, maybe much more. They might manage thousands of salespeople. Therefore, they can have considerable impact on your deal (and career). For those reasons alone, you want their buy-in as part of your dream team.

A perfect example of how executive buy-in can save the day happened with a deal I was working on at Adobe. Negotiations with the client had come down to the wire. It was the last day of the fourth quarter, which is as late as a deal can get without falling into the next fiscal year. The pressure was building to an immense level because the client was hedging about whether or not to commit to the deal.

The possibility of this household name brand client walking away at the last minute was becoming more and more likely, so I knew I needed a difference maker. That's when I decided it was the perfect time to bring in an executive named Steven Plous to seal the deal.

I needed someone with serious clout at Adobe to show our client how serious we were about ensuring their satisfaction. They were close to signing, but I could tell that they wanted verification that Adobe was going to do whatever it took to make them feel good about their partnership with us.

Steven immediately provided the peace of mind the client was looking for. He called into the meeting and told them, point-blank that he recognized the deal carried some risk for them and he would restructure it accordingly, but they needed to sign-off that day.

He totally defused the situation by easing the client's mind about their risk and making them understand that we wanted to do what was best for their company, as well as ours.

Even if you're working at a small company, top-tier executives—like Steven Plous—or board members can still move mountains for you.

Executives are much more likely to jump onboard with your dream team if you know how they like to contribute. Cater your approach to them based on their preference. For example, some executives don't like to get too deep into the weeds, while others relish that opportunity.

At a minimum, use the following three-step checklist when

engaging an executive to avoid any unproductive interactions. This will save you time and energy and enable the best possible results.

1. **Explain the desired meeting outcome**—The executive needs to know what you're trying to accomplish. Suppose you have a client in the travel industry, and you want to demonstrate your company's industry leadership by discussing how other clients in the same business have deployed your products. If you approach an executive to help and they decide they can't impact the outcome, they might delegate to someone else, which can be a great thing. Ideally, you want to match the desired outcome to the executive who is most capable of contributing to that potential meeting.

2. **Highlight the risk involved in the meeting**—Before the meeting, ensure the executive knows the risks involved, which may or may not be directly related to your deal. You might tell them, "Due to implementation issues on both sides, our product wasn't properly deployed two years ago. Now, the client is concerned that history will repeat itself if we move forward in new areas." This sort of disclaimer gives the executive exactly what he needs to know about any potential hot-button issues before talking with the client. If they know the risks involved, they'll be able to focus more intently on how they can help.

3. **Make an ask**—Once the executive understands the stakes of the game, they'll need to know specifically what they can do to help the situation. Making an ask might be as simple as something like saying, "To account for the problems they encountered with the previous implementation, and show them we're serious about preventing future issues..." If they're not comfortable with what you're asking, they'll

let you know, and you can determine some other ways they would be willing to assist.

Game Changer #52: Know how and when to pull executives in without creating unnecessary risk and wasted energy. Make an ask, highlight the risks, and define the outcome.

MVP EXTERNAL CONTACTS

Sometimes you need to look outside the organization to finish assembling your dream team. This section sheds a touch of light on how invaluable key external contacts can be in closing a deal. Remember, each deal is unique and may require unique resources from inside or outside the organization.

PARTNERS AND BUSINESS DEVELOPMENT

When I was working at IBM, I partnered with a business development leader from an outside company named Todd Underwood. He taught me how to use his company's visualization software to demonstrate how a soon-to-be built complex software solution across IBM and multiple partners would work for banking clients, without deploying a single line of code. That sort of thing may seem easy today, but it was positively disruptive in 2008.

To implement the actual software these companies wanted to see would have probably cost around $100 million in development resources and required a serious investment of time. With Todd's visualization piece, however, we were able to do it in a fraction of the normal timeframe and at no initial cost.

In this case, by bringing in the external party we were able to build a $150 million pipeline in record time, because the software visualization provided proof of how our solution would work for selected clients.

Superstar external parties like Todd and the innovative companies they come from are incredibly valuable, because they can collaborate on industry-shaping solutions for giant clients.

Turns out that Todd had much more access to IBM than I did, even though I worked for the company! When working with partners, you'll occasionally experience the same dynamic. One reason is that sometimes your partner contact who covers the client comes from the client itself.

For example, I met a managing director from Deloitte who owned an $85 million relationship with a major pharmaceutical company. Before Deloitte, he had worked at a pharma company he covered for twenty years in his previous role. The average salesperson is never going to be able to replicate that, but you can always discover ways to partner with people like that and share information.

Best of all, you can find these people on your own whereas most others aren't looking. Most salespeople get so wrapped up in the day-to-day, they don't seek out an external MVP contact like Todd. Thus, many reps miss the magic of working with them and reaping the associated rewards they can provide. It's always risky to bring in a third-party because it requires a tremendous amount of trust, faith, and the person's ability to execute. But the rewards of discovering a great one are well worth the risks.

THE CLIENT CHAMPION

Client champions will almost always emerge during a deal cycle. Incorporating these types of external contacts will provide unexpected benefits that come from an irreplaceable knowledge of the client environment. I remember having difficulty in finalizing the terms for a big deal I was trying to close with a giant in the financial services industry. The issue involved an unacceptable amount of credit risk that my team was requesting from a third party that was working closely with my client. Essentially, the third party would play a key role in funding the deal.

In that case, the client champion saved the deal by pushing the third party to pay the bill upfront. The third party was motivated to do so because of a confidential co-marketing arrangement. That eliminated the credit risk her finance department deemed as too great to proceed.

It sounds like a simple enough solution, but it's easy to get so locked in on these deals that the obvious answer can remain unseen. We wouldn't have thought of that as an option in a million years for the reasons of confidentiality surrounding the existence of the third-party arrangement, nobody else would have either...other than my client.

Think broadly when assembling your dream team. Cover a wide array of business expertise with top talent from all applicable areas of your organization. Get feedback and viewpoints from internal and external sources.

Once your dream team is comprehensive enough to go into battle, do a lot of brainstorming. Meet frequently to attack risk from all angles and create an optimal value proposition.

Make full use of everybody's unique strengths and support each other throughout the entire sales cycle. Be each other's champion and work together to achieve individual and team success.

Game Changer #53: When it comes to business partners, it's worth searching for the diamond in the rough. Look for industry expertise, a differentiated capability, or a trustworthy individual with a direct relationship to their CEO to get the job done.

WARNING SIGNS

When team leadership fails, warning signs can usually be found lurking. If appropriate action isn't taken soon enough, your deal could become the victim of a singularly-threaded solution, lack of good communication, a failing team member, or poor internal selling among other forms of team-related, deal-killing dilemmas.

Learn how to recognize some of the most common problems quickly, so there will be plenty of time for working with your team to correct them before they become deal-killers.

A SINGLE-THREADED APPROACH

Successful teams usually develop multiple client stakeholders in pursuit of a deal, rather than relying on a single-threaded approach where the team is funneled through one point of contact with the client.

A single-threaded dysfunction can also happen when the team

is myopically focused on a specific feature, benefit, or product at a time without properly considering or explaining the full solution, which could present opportunities for a larger deal or several additional deals. Any form of a single threaded approach usually leads to suboptimal results.

 Game Changer #54: Don't be single-threaded in your approach. Make sure the team is exploring all options for a solution to meet the holistic needs of the client.

COMMUNICATION BOTTLENECKS

Some people keep too much information to themselves, rather than sharing knowledge that could improve the team's chances to excel. Everybody on the team needs to know what's going on with the client and what the next steps will be.

Even if you're not the front person on a deal team, encourage open communication up and down the lineup. The more often people are having informative interactions with each other about the deal pursuit, the easier everybody's job will be, and it will foster trust. That way, nobody feels like they've been left on an island.

PROBLEMATIC TEAM MEMBERS

Trust among team members is critical. It allows for more independent action, inspires ownership, and enables people to ask for help in supporting their own areas of weakness. The team leader must do everything possible to maintain that positive vibe. Despite a leader's best efforts, however, an individual may operate on their own terms without thought for the broader team, creating a threat to team morale and effectiveness.

Whether or not you're the team's leader, you should assume responsibility to redirect the efforts of a team member who may not be fully invested in the deal. Apply one of the lessons you learned about having tough conversations in this situation, and show them how their assistance will not only be in their own best interest but also that of the team and the company.

Game Changer #55: Occasionally, you may run into a weak link on your team or an individual that actively causes problems. Nothing good will come from calling them out or embarrassing them, but keeping them onboard could compound the disruption and damage morale. Find a way to discreetly manage them away from your dream team.

POOR INTERNAL SELLING

Closing a big deal requires buy-in from a lot of internal stakeholders. Ensure all parties understand what the vision of customer success looks like on every deal.

Internal selling can be much more involved than you might expect. In fact, I've heard many top salespeople describe it as the most challenging aspect of their role. Having a large team to address the needs of each client can be a tremendous resource on which to lean. However, it can also add complexity. The more team members you have, the more opinions for solutions you'll have, and the more formal approvals you'll need to get things done.

As the team leader, you'll need to be adept at communicating effectively to solicit the necessary buy-in from all the right personnel.

Poor internal selling usually results in a deal not getting the support it needs regarding resources, contract support, legal support, or validation of the deal structure.

THE DEAL TEAM CHECKLIST

- Develop relationships with deal support, legal, product, etc. as soon as you start at your new company.
- Bring in someone who is exceptional in your areas of weakness.
- Shore up the weaknesses on your team by using everyone's strengths to support each other.
- Create an environment of trust with open communication.
- Bring in executives, matching their desire to contribute with the outcome you're looking to achieve. Then, highlight the risks, and make an ask.
- Meet regularly to brainstorm solutions to risks and strengthen your plans for action.
- Seek out innovative companies that are excited to partner with you to create new solutions to your clients' problems.
- Avoid the warning signs of dysfunction, such as: a single-threaded approach, communications breakdown, misaligned intra-team incentives, and poor internal selling.

The key takeaway from this chapter is to realize how much of a team sport the game of sales really is. Although you should always hold yourself accountable for the end results, you don't have to do it alone. In fact, you shouldn't. Take the time to get to know great people inside and outside the organization who can help you to close deals smoother, faster, and bigger.

In the next chapter, we'll discuss how to capture hidden value. This skill will uncover benefits for both you and your clients. It will become an indispensable resource. This is also the last piece of information before we conclude with my thoughts on how to look for, create, and close mega deals!

CHAPTER 11

CAPTURING HIDDEN VALUE

"Facts which at first seem improbable will, even with scant exploration, drop the cloak which has hidden them."
—GALILEO GALILEI (ENGINEER, PHYSICIST, ASTRONOMER)

An abundance of sales books preaching the old-school gospel of hardball tactics, smarmy manipulation, and overly complex analysis have already been written. Unfortunately, these dysfunctional methods cause far more harm than good in today's game of sales. In my experience, they create a divide between opposing forces, rather than an amicable partnership that benefits both sides, potentially for many years to come.

Instead of treating a sales deal like some sort of mixed martial arts event, where each side uses various kicks, punches, and strangle holds to force the other into submission, try the easier, friendlier, and far more productive method of *capturing hidden value.*

Before you can begin to apply this refreshing concept, it helps to know a specific and purposeful definition of what value really is. I consider value to be anything—tangible or intangible—that improves the potential outcome of the deal for the client. This might seem extremely cut and dry, but in reality, many forms of value are hidden and need to be uncovered for optimal results.

There are several reasons why value can be hidden:

- Having an unclear, inaccurate, or incomplete understanding of the problems the client is facing.
- A lack of flexibility in applying sales messaging provided by marketing that doesn't tailor the deal to the client's specific situation.
- Becoming overly focused on hard metrics like return on investment (ROI) without understanding or going deeply enough into the assumptions behind the numbers to translate and present the metrics in a uniquely meaningful way to the client.
- Allowing procurement to direct and define a deal path.
- Technical issues or internal challenges become all consuming.

Assuming you've already done your homework—as outlined in chapter 2—to understand the industry and technology landscape, and you've implemented a framework like the ValuePrompter® to get to the root of the client's problems, you may still need to uncover sources of value to get the deal done.

Sources of value are unmet client wants or needs that may exist. Some of these value sources may be fairly obvious, but others may be hidden due to one of the reasons I mentioned in the previous bulleted list.

UNCOVERING VALUE

By exploring creative ways to resolve each client's problems, you'll unlock the pathway to uncovering value. These possibilities for hidden value must then be prioritized and translated into the client's terms at both the individual and corporate level to avoid any miscommunication.

Game Changer #56: The more complex the transaction, the more energy you should expend on capturing hidden value.

As you pursue each deal, potential sources of value will be translated and prioritized in unexpected ways. You'll find that uncovering differences in perspective around them is one of the most rewarding and exciting aspects of sales.

Don't get stuck on any single item. Maintain flexibility in how you label and prioritize your list. This mapping exercise is critical to ensuring your client realizes value on the purchase while preserving your own deal value as well.

The following is a generic list of value sources I've used in the past, along with examples of each so you can visualize how to get to value-based solutions. This list is not comprehensive, but you can use it as an effective kick-starter to create your own list.

- **Additional Revenue**—Collaborate with your client on a spreadsheet that covers all the numbers and steps involved in achieving a satisfactory return on investment.
- **Cost Savings**—Demonstrate why your product is cheaper

than the alternative. Show how your product eliminates costs by creating more efficient processes or replaces expensive service arrangements.

- **Time Savings**—Show your client how automation or more easily accessible data can free up their time to focus on other aspects of their job.
- **Risk Reduction**—Explain how your solution reduces some form of organizational risk for your client. Define how your product is more stable than their current solution or how it will reduce the rate of contract cancellations.
- **Regulatory Change**—Describe how your product has assisted other clients in meeting upcoming regulatory requirements. Discuss a plan with your client to do the same for them.
- **Corporate Transactions**—Prime the client's environment for an initial public offering (IPO), merger integration, or divestiture.
- **Partnerships**—Assist your client in getting more out of an existing partnership. This could be any partnership, such as consulting, co-marketing, or a channel partnership that directly impacts revenue.
- **Personal Interest**—Brainstorm a way to benefit your specific client contact. Maybe you know how to solve a nagging business problem for them that could clear a pathway to a promotion.
- **Training**—Develop a training schedule, onsite and remote sessions, webinars, online training, and access to top consultants.
- **Access**—Set up a meeting with your company's C-level executives to prove to your client how important their partnership is to your team. Provide reference discussions or speaking engagements at your company or at industry events.

- **Resource Alignment**—Deploy experts who have implemented similar successful solutions before, rather than newbies who might need to learn on the job.

I kept a visualization of that list in my head and used it to guide my approach with a client who was experiencing significant pain with their email personalization program. They didn't see a way out, which presented me with an opportunity to help. By prioritizing the sources of value and discussing it with them in their language, I was able to help them understand the fit of my company's solution.

First, I explained to them how they could get more out of a key partnership. An existing consulting firm was failing them in the area of email personalization, and they couldn't be replaced due to an existing contract.

I suggested a thorough training program to coincide with our implementation. By doing so, they would be assured that 100,000 personalized emails per month would be delivered that would preserve a $25 million annual revenue stream. Additionally, they could achieve cost savings by eliminating $5 million in marketing automation, services, and training overages in the following year when that contract was scheduled to be reviewed.

After prioritizing partnership and cost savings as sources of value, I introduced the potential for time savings. The client was spending far too much time putting out fires caused by using an outdated product. Putting out fires wasn't the only time waster involved. They were also spending an inordinate amount of time in meetings on incoming fix requests to manage the situation. By switching over to our more intuitive product, they were positioned to cut up to 50 percent of that time.

The final item on my prioritization value source list for that client was risk reduction. That client was also about to launch a new $10 million global CRM project. I described how our new solution would integrate seamlessly with that project, which gave them a peace of mind that served as icing on our cake of hidden value.

That scenario is a typical way to capture hidden value for a client. There's nothing overly complex about it. By creating your own similar, prioritized list, you're simply creating a system for proving the value of your solutions to your clients.

 Game Changer #57: Some sources of value may be common across clients, yet there are always new interpretations, prioritizations, and sources for you to discover. Each deal has its own unique value fingerprint.

Common sources of value for the broader team and organization are time savings, cost savings, incremental revenue, regulatory reform, and risk reduction. Some sources of hidden value can be uncovered by focusing on the professional gain for the individual executive. Others exist, but it's up to you to have conversations with your clients that stretch to a more personal, trusted advisor level to find them. (If you're wondering how to achieve the desirable status of trusted advisor, turn back to chapter 2 and take notes on how to build credibility with executives.)

Capturing hidden value involves not only a prioritized list of potential sources, but also requires the mentality to analyze, brainstorm, and discuss various ways to track down value for all your clients. Consider the following guidelines to maintain such a mentality.

- To unlock the greatest value possible in your client relationships, keep the long-term vision of the partnership in mind during your interactions.
- Always aim for a fair deal that benefits both parties. That way, your clients will immediately sense your good intentions and be much more likely to share ideas. Otherwise, key information that could have made the difference between deal success and failure will remain hidden due to the guarded nature of your clients.
- Avoid approaching conversations about value in a prescriptive manner. Instead, use a hypothesis-based approach to make a list of sources of value for both sides (we'll talk about this in more detail in the next section). Remember, what you might interpret as valuable may be of little importance to your client and vice-versa. With that in mind, identify items that don't matter much to you but matter a lot to the other party and vice-versa. Work through both lists to see where each side can assist the other side in expanding the value of the deal. This activity shows how the deal pie is often times capable of growth.
- Keep the conversation going, even if all hope seems lost. With continuing discourse, you have a chance to eventually stumble upon a mutually beneficial idea.
- When explaining value to the client, use their language and metrics. Otherwise, the meaning of your efforts will go unnoticed.

In each deal, there will be at least one source of value (or the way that items of value are prioritized) that will surprise you and may never occur again. Another surprise may be in how far you can expand the value you've created or uncovered. I like to call this *growing the pie* because bigger deals come from not taking a bigger piece of the same-sized pie, but by making a bigger pie for everyone involved.

GROWING THE PIE

I attended a popular class at Google that solidified the concepts I and others were naturally applying to capturing hidden value.

Not only did that class prove to be a deep breath of fresh air, where the instructor encouraged the idea of collaboration over playing hardball, but he also spoke at length about how sometimes the best value to be created is *invisible*—aka *hidden.*

The instructor, Stuart Diamond, is a world-renowned expert on negotiation, although the term negotiation doesn't accurately describe his expertise in my opinion. He talks more about *growing the pie* for all involved parties, which means he isn't explaining how to get the other side to give you a higher percentage of the deal. Instead, he talks about how both parties should work together to make the pie bigger for everyone involved.

This is really the heart of what I'm hoping to impress upon you with this chapter. Many salespeople have been searching for hidden value, whether they realize it or not. The distinguishing aspect of this approach, however, is an intentional focus on growing the pie for all parties. It's not about taking a larger slice for only yourself. Rather, I urge you to find a secret stash of ingredients to make the entire pie bigger, so you and your client can enjoy more delicious outcomes.

In that class, Stuart cited an example from a deal where Google was offering a small advertising client the ability to leverage Google Cloud (in early beta stage), mostly out of a good faith effort to show the client that Google appreciated their business. (Keep in mind, I had nothing to do with this deal. It is simply a case study, executed by someone else, which was expounded upon in a classroom setting.) What Google didn't realize was that the client had an extraordinary need for the cloud service, and that simple good faith gesture of caring resulted in a $20 million cloud contract.

The hidden value in that simple act of good faith was even bigger than the monetary amount of the contract, because the relationship was immediately up-leveled to the C-suite. This gave the client a direct line of communication to more effectively articulate to the CEO and board meaningful ways Google could drive value through increased advertising investment as well.

That case study served as a prime example of two critical, value-centric elements:

- That Google team exemplified the importance of choosing adding value over hardball negotiation.
- By simply doing what was best for their client, they unearthed hidden value that paid off in a big way; the perfect win-win scenario.

That example should also not be misinterpreted as a stroke of sales genius. The large contract and the resulting additional value of the deal were revealed organically by caring enough about the client to do the right thing. It was a simple act of serendipity that enabled the pie to grow bigger for everyone involved, which is emblematic of one of the guidelines I listed previously for creating hidden value.

Game Changer #58: By focusing on abundance and expanding the pie vs. scarcity and zero-sum game, you dramatically increase your chances of capturing hidden value.

Recommended Resource: *Getting More* by Stuart Diamond.

Follow the guidelines and keep your eyes open to maximize your potential for creating hidden value. By having the correct mindset and approach to your client relationships, you will increase the odds of serendipity working in your favor.

Going outside your role and product are two key actions that will grow the pie and expand your prioritized list of hidden value.

Shun the idea of *staying in your lane*. Instead, look holistically at the organization for which you're working. That wide-angle lens could provide an opportunity for you to make a big difference internally, which can only improve your ability to close bigger and better deals more often.

GOING OUTSIDE YOUR ROLE

Being confident enough to go outside your role enables you to have a bigger impact on your organization. Now, I'd like to share a story about how this happened for me when I worked at Google, so you can search for similar opportunities at your organization.

Years ago, I was in a position to help our clients take better advantage of digital advertising, which was just starting to take off. The goal wasn't just to sell ads on websites or alongside YouTube videos, because those things were useless to our clients unless their organizations knew how to adopt and analyze the impact that digital could have on their business.

I realized that this uncertainty around digital was an issue that made it difficult for our clients to maximize the value of leads generated through their advertising programs. At the time, this aligned with the rest of the B2B industry, where most clients didn't truly understand the value of digital to drive their business.

Although striving to educate about 20 percent of our client base on the power of digital, was clearly not in my job description, I knew it was a gap that needed to be filled, and if Google could provide that missing link, everyone involved would receive tremendous benefits. Therefore, it seemed appropriate for me to step outside my role in that situation.

Once we began to focus on the problem, we discovered that startlingly few sales-driven organizations were adept at leveraging digital technology in general. Clients were struggling mightily with the transformation process from whatever legacy systems and processes they were using.

Moreover, most sales teams had been comfortable with relying on offline sales tactics exclusively for many years. At best, salespeople were skeptical of leads generated from online sources. At worst, they ignored the leads completely. Significant organizational change and learning would be required to solve these problems. I figured we could start by hosting a digital transformation session for one of our clients to help them advance their marketing and sales efforts.

Shortly after, I turned inspiration into action and sat down with the senior director of digital to arrive at a plan for the digital transformation session. He immediately got onboard with the idea, and we began the process of scheduling the event.

When the day came, the CMO kicked off the session with a few state-of-the-state ideas; some high-level topics that everybody could relate to. Then, the director spoke about the importance of digital. After that, I appeared on stage and talked about some of the best and most recent innovations from our company and the rest of the industry. I also presented a clear picture of how the clients' company and others would advance in the coming year.

Sitting down with the director to plan a day like that was definitely going outside of my day-to-day role and so was getting on stage as a follow-up to those high-level executives. It was an amazing experience and I'm so glad I did it. I was on stage in front of hundreds of people and broadcast globally, so it gave Google great exposure. Besides that, it felt great to help drive impactful change at a multi-billion-dollar company, and get the entire organization more excited and engaged in digital.

Our partnership experienced a significant increase in business with that particular client as a result of that event. Their organization became better prepared and more focused on getting value from their efforts at digital.

Based on the success of that experience, we replicated that event for several other clients to get the attention of hundreds of other marketing and sales leaders. Hosting these events became a core part of our overall approach to the nascent world of connecting online and offline marketing and sales efforts.

By creating that initial event, I stepped outside my role, which expanded the value for that and future clients via training, enhanced internal partnerships, and ROI, fully translated into their language.

As you go outside your role, discuss your client's organizational problems broadly, even if you don't think your offering is directly related to any of them. Your clients will naturally become comfortable partnering with you, because they'll realize you're not a sales robot. Rather, they'll think of you as a multi-dimensional problem solver and valuable consultant to their business.

GOING OUTSIDE YOUR PRODUCT

Thinking more holistically about your product is another way to establish to yourself as a consultant to your client.

When you consider the specific deal on which you're working, it may be a small blip on the radar of your company and the client's. That's why it helps to have a bigger mindset than that myopic level of thinking. Chances are, each company has multiple product lines, which means there could be numerous opportunities to build bridges that bring the two companies together.

Create a grid when thinking about the various ways to create a fruitful partnership. The grid should include your company, the client's company, your solution for the current deal, and several third-party stakeholders. From there, identify value exchanges between the companies. To make the most comprehensive map possible, ask yourself some questions that stimulate brainstorming.

- What are the value exchanges?
- How are the two companies currently working together?
- What operational changes might result from the proposed solution?
- Who will be involved, even tangentially, from both companies and third parties?
- What complimentary products might be influenced by the proposed solution?

By going outside your product, you can also spin off multiple smaller deals to address other issues the client may have not even realized they had.

For example, when I worked for IBM in 2006, I was assigned the task of selling thousands of smartphones per transaction to the enterprise on behalf of a client.

The immediate need was to create and support a pilot that could run basic email, contact, and calendaring software. Two issues, however, existed as barriers to that goal.

- This was the first smartphone on the market. Everything to that point was Blackberry, so we were in unchartered territory. An original and creative solution was needed to accomplish our task.
- The smartphones were married to cost-prohibitive, two-year contracts, which made a ninety-day pilot virtually impossible to execute.

The newness of the product made the problems we were facing unprecedented. Therefore, going outside my product was the only way a solution was going to be achieved. With that in mind, we thought, "Maybe we can work with a service provider to see if they can help eliminate the barrier of a two-year contract for the pilot."

My next meeting was with Verizon to see if they would be willing to collaborate on such a project. After a few friendly exchanges, we arrived at a deal that would provide value for all stakeholders. We suggested a ninety-day plan for pilot participants to essentially beta test the devices and unlock the potential of smartphone technology for large organizations. Meanwhile, Verizon received substantial value from the partnership as well, because the pilot created the potential for thousands of new user contracts for their enterprise team. Overall, getting this pilot provision from Verizon was a huge win.

First of all, with a ninety-day plan now available to us, we acquired the ability to sell something that otherwise would have been prohibitively expensive and dramatically reduced the risk associated with the pilot program.

Even more importantly, our pilot program enabled us to build the first smartphone ecosystem by recruiting software providers to handle basic banking and news delivery on the devices. We also defined what the corporate governance structure for these programs would look like. Our approach created massive value that almost nobody saw before we stepped outside the product to form an enterprise-grade solution.

We opened up a new world of possibilities in that situation, by both expanding and creating sources of value for all involved. Keep in mind, however, if you're planning to use a similar approach on a barrier to something you're currently working on, I advise caution, because your pipeline can get so big that you need to bring in other salespeople to help you manage it. What a great problem to have!

CONVERSATION, NOT NEGOTIATION

As you walk away from this chapter, remember that creating value is all about realizing negotiation is not where the game of sales is won and lost today. A friendlier approach is what will foster relationships, encourage more conversation, and help to capture hidden value, which will make the deal bigger and better for you and your client.

Remember, you're not going to have all the answers to a client's wish list upfront; nobody does. Sources are found only by consistent discovery and hypothesis-driven testing. Something is there on every client interaction. It could be around time-saving measures, process efficiencies, payment terms, revenue-centric variables. It's a matter of keeping all the guidelines mentioned at the beginning of this chapter in mind and checking off each box as you explore them with your client. Talk about all the sources of value with your client, starting with the most valuable. Inevitably, the deal pie will get bigger, which will make everyone happier in the long run.

Engage in conversations, probe deeply with questions, and always have the goal of doing what's best for both parties at the forefront of your deal process. By performing those simple tasks, hidden value will become visible to you.

Once you're fully awakened to the idea of capturing hidden value, and you're comfortable with the other principles you've learned about so far, you should be well-prepared to seek, create, and close mega deals, which is what the next chapter is all about.

CHAPTER 12

MEGA-DEALS

"If people aren't calling you crazy, you aren't thinking big enough."
—RICHARD BRANSON (BUSINESS MAGNATE,
INVESTOR, AUTHOR, PHILANTHROPIST)

Identifying an exceptionally large deal is similar to capturing hidden value because the mega deal is invisible at the beginning of the process. You need to be looking for the opportunity to create one.

The mega-deal I'm talking about is any deal that is unusually large for your company and likely stretches the existing go-to market approach.

The dollar value of a "mega-deal" can vary greatly depending on the organization. It could be as little as $1 million or much more. Classification depends on what constitutes a *large deal* for your company.

Mega-deals are all about the offer.

You need to graduate your mindset from thinking about deals

on a transactional level to deals with a little more impact, all the way up to an offer that is *big and bold*.

Start thinking about ways to stretch the limits of what's been done before at your company grounded in items of interest to the client that have major impact.

Always think big with your offer!

THINK BIGGER!

A particularly decisive moment reminded me to push my thought process forward to think bigger. I was flying to Los Angeles for a big client meeting. A bunch of people from Adobe were going to be there, business partners and numerous attendees from the client.

The purpose of the meeting was to discuss the client's overall strategy and how we could help. Going into the meeting it seemed there was a segment of one of our products our team could plug-in to make for a quick win. Almost no work would be involved, and the add-on was a no-brainer. But was that really in the best interest of all parties? I thought it would be like throwing a pebble in the ocean, relative to the larger problem.

As I was considering such an obvious and easy plug-in, I realized how the whole idea of a quick win seemed like the easy way out. It was a sure thing and that could be the end of it, but I couldn't help but feel like it wasn't the best thing to do. After all, we're in sales because it is a challenging and rewarding way to make a living, not to go through the motions.

As I was thinking how that deal wasn't going to provide any

meaningful impact for any of us—not the client, the business partners, or my company—I started to reflect upon a commonality between all the larger deals I had closed in my career to that point.

It occurred to me that I had thought big about all those deals. Rather than accepting the transactional limits, I went into the sales cycle with bigger thoughts. I began my approach in those situations not with a product to plug-in, so I could walk away quickly, but with visions of solving a big problem.

REPEATEDLY REFINE YOUR OFFER

When you find your mega deal, mental toughness is required to work your way through the long and complex sales cycle. Expect there are several points in each mega-deal where things seem to be on the verge of falling apart. When that happens, if you're not mentally prepared, the deal could dissolve.

Game Changer #61: Mega deals will "die" several times along the way. Don't panic. Regroup with your team, form a plan, and re-engage with your client.

Constructing a solid offer with confidence in its ability to drive a solution to a major business challenge for your client will go a long way to strengthening your resolve. With that in mind, a good offer—small, medium, or large—requires a lot of pieces to be put in place, which we may take for granted during a transactional deal. A solid offer includes most of the following items:

- Contract
- Technology
- People
- Plan
- Value you've defined
- The unique vision that only you, your company, and partners can deliver

A mega-deal encompasses *all* those things. Not only that, the offer needs to fit perfectly within your client's timelines, as well as their people, partners, technology, contractual obligations, and their ability to pay. Those things need to fit together, and to secure a mega deal, requires consistent attention to detail in all those areas.

If you're going to think big, which you should, your offer needs to match that ambition. You should ensure your bases are covered by consistently iterating on the elements of your offer until you've arrived at one that meets all the various obstacles, challenges, and requirements with which you've been presented. It is only through iterating on the offer, in partnership with your client, where you can break new ground.

PERSPECTIVE ON SCALE

It's important to not let the complexity associated with mega-deals scare you off. When compared to a mergers and acquisitions (M&A), the mega-deals we're talking about here are relatively small. Selling or buying a company involves exponentially more levels of complexity than any product or solution-based deal.

So many more things need to be considered in an M&A. There

are likely consultants, teams of lawyers, and numerous commercial relationships that all need to be covered, as well as hundreds or even thousands of people. When companies are bought and sold, $50 billion or more could be at stake.

Comparatively, a $10 million mega-deal is a grain of sand on the beach. Sometimes it helps to think of things at scale to maintain a healthy mindset and stay motivated, rather than becoming unnecessarily overwhelmed by a transaction with a larger than normal dollar amount.

When thinking about the grand scheme of things, you start to realize that mega-deals of any size are achievable. Sure, more variables and greater risk are involved versus what you experience in closing simpler, transactional deals. But mega-deals also provide exponentially increased rewards, both financially and professionally.

Closing a mega-deal is an exceptional feeling. I can only imagine it's like playing on a championship team, where the players support each other and complement everyone's skill sets by design. Similarly, to close a mega-deal, you'll need to collaborate with your deal team to a level of supreme efficiency.

When all those moving parts of an organization work in sync with each other to produce a mega-deal, it's a magnificent outcome. Of course, to make it happen, you'll need to break new ground of some sort at the organization for which you're working. To close a mega-deal requires flexibility and persistence in how you formulate your offer.

If you're selling for a technology company, they give you the product, service, messaging, pricing, contract structure etc.

If you live within that box, there are all sorts of rules that will tie you down, which sometimes are a good thing because they can help you to streamline your pipeline of deals. With mega-deals, however, you're going to have to know when and how to step out of that box, and how far beyond the box you can go.

You need to find what the client needs and possibly create a much larger deal than the one currently being discussed. Otherwise, you could end up missing a big need that your client might get fulfilled by a competitor.

MEGA-DEAL MELTDOWN

My first year at Adobe featured a particularly gut-wrenching development when defeat was snatched from the jaws of victory. My team and I were about to close a seven-figure deal with a large client. This company wanted to transition their entire advertising operations. Our company had the perfect platform to match their specific structure and technology footprint, except for one minor detail.

The client was about to schedule a call to make the announcement that they were switching to our platform, but they cancelled it at the last minute because we couldn't manage a certain aspect of their campaigns.

Technically, it was a relatively minor social platform that our service team could not manage, because there was an added layer of contracting and due diligence, and we decided we couldn't support it.

I checked and re-checked with my team and they confirmed

that it was not something we could turn around in the necessary timeframe.

In hindsight, I was not aggressive enough in double-checking all the boxes of my offer. I should have recognized the platform as a must-have business requirement for the client, even though they themselves shrugged it off. Also, although I knew our people had the capability of managing what the client was asking, the deal progressed too quickly for us to react in time. In the end, the deal fell to a competitor who could cover the full gambit without delay.

The client didn't expect any provider would be able to cover everything, but once they realized our competition could, it changed their perspective.

Afterward, I became determined to make sure a similar problem would never happen again, so I reflected deeply on where that deal went south.

I realized that I wasn't pre-aligned closely enough with the product management and services teams needed to handle that outlier situation. Moreover, the expansive nature of our offer fell somewhat outside the lines of our standard go-to-market product offering from a timing and delivery perspective.

Game Changer #62: Thinking big about your offer requires thinking big about all the variables involved.

Game Changer #63: It's imperative to be as thorough as possible to make sure your offer is sound, because there will be surprises anytime you push the established boundaries.

After some self-analysis, I took steps to make sure I didn't repeat any of the same mistakes. Soon after, I refocused my energy to work on the next mega-deal opportunity.

MEGA-DEAL REDEMPTION

Shortly after the social platform setback happened, I applied the lessons learned from it to attempt a mega-deal with a bank that was worth more than twice the value of the mega-deal meltdown.

This client is an elite and well-known bank. They were looking to shift focus from a business to business institution to engage with millions of individual customers directly. This presented them with a monumental challenge, which translated to a tremendous opportunity. Millions or even billions of dollars were at stake for them during this transformation, but with the right pieces in place for a great offer, my company had the chance to move the needle for them in a big way.

When the time came to show the client how we could build a bridge to where they wanted to go, this time I left nothing to chance.

Sitting in a room with ten people from the client side going through all the details around services, technology, and campaign launch schedule, I knew that I was beyond meticulous ensuring all the offer details were tied together and attainable.

To illustrate the intricate process involved with closing the deal:

- Our team and I began with a discovery and general education phase. For the first six to eight months, we built a strategic foundation and gained a thorough understanding of their operational challenges.
- From October to December, we focused on advertising operations and the surrounding processes and initiatives.
- From January to March, we concentrated on executive alignment up to and including the CMO. We agreed on high-level budget and pricing parameters.
- From March to April, we scoped the focus of the deal and iterated on a mutual plan with the client to close before the end of May. We also met with all related teams to validate our approach.
- From April to May, we collaborated with their implementation team, partners, legal, and compliance, and completed negotiations on special terms and pricing.

That's a rough timeline. There was a lot of parallel processing that occurred as well. During the final stage of the deal, we went through commercial terms and campaign evaluation. We also discussed the best way to execute their advertising program and identified technology gaps to cover with a subcontractor.

What made the offer special was its broad scope, customized fit for the client, and the simplicity in how it could be described from both a commercial and benefits perspective.

Through rigorous analysis of the offer's many complex components, we were also able to tie everything together into a single compelling price point. Furthermore, there weren't any surprise add-ons or last-minute *gotchas* that the team couldn't handle thanks to the effort we put into firming up all the details of our offer.

Overall, the offer led to a large transaction with a mountain of value behind it, validated at every level of the organization. It gave the client full transparency into their campaign performance and costs, ownership of their data, integration across both marketing and advertising technology, and a platform-based approach to continuously evolve their marketing focus from B2B to B2C, so they could accelerate the growth of their business.

To ensure we could get everything deployed on time and without incident, we implemented upgrade plans for analytics and data management functions that support advertising operations. In addition, we reviewed services strategy, operating processes, and technical set-up.

In the end, we covered all our bases in that deal. We were meticulous with our planning, but most importantly, we implemented a contractual framework I referred to as a pass-through model, which allowed us to present a comprehensive offer by having a subcontracted, embedded agency as part of our team to cover any gaps we had in technology or service. That enabled Adobe to manage the overall advertising budget, while partnering with the client to drive their overall strategy.

START AT THE TOP OF THE OFFER CASCADE

During the creation of that offer, I spotted an opportunity to turn what might have been a small deal into something much bigger.

The mega-deal process begins with breaking down each opportunity into one of four tiers of deals, which is represented by the associated "Offer Cascade" graphic.

OFFER CASCADE

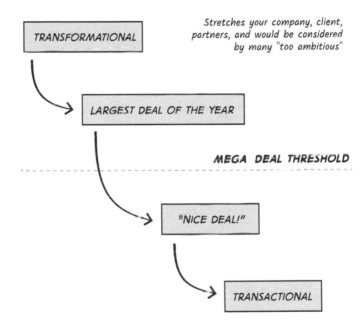

KNOW THE DETAILS OF EACH OFFER AND START AT THE TOP.
WORK YOUR WAY DOWN AS NEEDED.

TRANSFORMATIONAL

Stretches your company, client, partners, and would be considered by many "too ambitious"

LARGEST DEAL OF THE YEAR

MEGA DEAL THRESHOLD

"NICE DEAL!"

TRANSACTIONAL

Starting here will reduce your chances of closing a mega deal

You want to start your thinking not at the transactional level, but at the transformational level. Think big at the start. If you discover that the deal is something less than one of the two or three largest of the year, that's fine. That's exactly where a lot of deals finish, but approach everything with the idea that the sky is the limit. Then, level down if necessary.

1. Transformational deals require a tremendous effort, teamwork, and can account for millions of dollars. These deals are so big and bold, few salespeople think about them. Many of those who do, might be too uneasy with the increased variables and levels of complexity to propose something of this magnitude. Others might allow self-doubt to stop them from presenting their genuinely great ideas to create one. Don't let fear of complexity or self-doubt stop you. A simple change of mindset from misplaced anxiety to thinking big about the offer provides the foundation for creating these deals. Keep in mind, however, these deals are difficult to create and they're not always there. Don't force it, but you have nothing to lose by starting the pursuit here and working your way down.

2. The next tier from the top are still large deals that require considerable focus, but they're not quite as complex or time consuming. If this is where your deal lands, you'll have given yourself a chance at closing the largest deal of the year for your company.

3. Level three deals are less creative and mostly standard, go-to-market opportunities. If this is what serves your client best, then do what's right for them and close the deal. But you should always aim higher and hope to create more value for both companies if possible.

4. Transactional deals are usually in the tens of thousands of dollars or low six figures. They're the most commonly sought after deals by newer salespeople. This is the starting point for a lot of salespeople, but I urge you to flip that model and start at the transformational level. Incrementally work your way down to this level if that's all that exists.

The reality is a lot of salespeople—me included at times—don't always feel comfortable going for mega-deals or even the second tier of the offer cascade. There are a lot of reasons why this may be the case.

Perhaps you see the formal approvals needed from management to secure mega-deals as insurmountable barriers, or you might feel more confident by taking a smaller deal off the table. I encourage you to move past those thoughts. Why not shoot for the moon?

TRUST YOUR INSTINCTS

Thinking big about your offer is the foundation of creating mega-deals. So be ready to capitalize when you spot the opportunity for a mega-deal. Do not, however, force a mega-deal where one doesn't exist. That will only result in making the client feel like you're not listening to their needs. Instead, be aware of the biggest of possibilities in each deal, but in the end, trust your instincts about what the right deal looks like for your client.

If you're working on a deal that doesn't cross the mega-deal threshold, and it's impossible to create anything more from it, that's okay. Feel free to push the limits and do everything you can to create the most value for everyone involved, but in the end, you need to do what's best for the client in every situation. If the best thing for them is to focus your attention on getting a highly transactional deal closed in a timely manner, do it. You can always revisit the situation later if you find a much bigger problem to solve.

If at some point you spot that a mega-deal is possible, however, you must understand that mega-deals involve mega-risk. They can stretch the organization far beyond its comfort zone, so be prepared to be challenged by your internal support teams and executives.

Relationships can be strained as a result of the increased stress and pressure. You could run into anything from compatibility problems with technology to implementation issues. Mega-deals may require you to bring the company into unfamiliar territory. That's why it's critically important to be diligent in your deal planning.

Having support from all the key players, including top-tier executives, is required for pushing organizational limits. Work with the C-suite of the client's company and articulate how your offer can add significant value to their entire organization. Iterate and refine terms as you go.

If you're thinking comprehensively about your offer, you'll be able to match the terms to your client's biggest problems. Some of those issues may have been previously unknown to the client. Sometimes, they need help identifying the changes they need to make. It's important to partner with them on their investigation. You can make a massive impact by working with them to not just solve a tactical issue (which is fine, if that's all there is to it) but to create a big-picture vision for change.

You have all the resources necessary to find, create, and close your first mega-deal, so think big and go for it!

CONCLUSION

"We are what we repeatedly do. Excellence, then, is not an act but a habit."

—ARISTOTLE (GREEK PHILOSOPHER)

A lot of what you just read may seem counterintuitive, especially the ideas of steering toward risk and having tough conversations early. In the beginning, you may struggle with implementing some of these ideas. After all, setbacks will find even the best of us throughout the course of our lives. Setbacks are inevitable, and you can't grow without them.

Throughout your career, you'll encounter multitudes of decision points regarding the management of your pipeline and the use of different frameworks. You'll need to have tough conversations and you'll have an occasional horrible meeting. Furthermore, you'll need to find value where it's not readily apparent. It can be daunting to keep searching for that value, but you need to believe in your abilities and persevere.

The dark side of sales will test your resolve from time to time. Hopefully, this book has armed you with good advice and go-to tips for how to best handle those situations. Before long, your odds of finding and enjoying the long and winding road of success will significantly increase.

Sales success can be achieved with many different approaches by many different personality types. Remember if I can do it, so can you. I don't think there's anything inherently special about my ability to close deals, but I have learned some invaluable lessons over the years about caring, risk, and resilience. If only I knew about all these things when I first started out, I could have had a twenty-year head start in my career. Then again, that's why I wrote this book. I want you to have what I didn't. Take these lessons to heart and get a jump on your own success.

Now that you've finished reading about the lessons I've learned from working at Adobe, Amazon, Google, and IBM, I challenge you to apply one idea from this book the next time you're at work. Maybe you should work on building a solid pipeline. Perhaps you want to look into Value Selling. Or maybe it's time to get to work on that mega-deal. Whatever you choose, have fun with it. The game of sales really is an awesome experience, but it's up to you to make the most of it.

APPENDIX A

GAME CHANGERS

Game Changer #1: Enterprise sales is an elite profession with significant lateral and upward mobility. Outside of executive leadership, the highest earners at most companies, large and small, are the top salespeople.

Game Changer #2: Closing a deal is one of the most exciting experiences in business. Each time you make it happen, you'll learn how to do it bigger, better, and faster.

Game Changer #3: Sales will allow you to meet and even work with the top business leaders in the world.

Game Changer #4: Top enterprise salespeople are teammates, consultants, analysts, product experts, project managers, and leaders. How do you stack up in these areas?

Game Changer #5: Track the leaders of your chosen industry or vertical. Notice what's unique about their product lines, go-to market approaches, and their internal as well as external investments. If publicly traded, review 10-K sections one and seven for business overview and key financial performance metrics respectively.

Game Changer #6: By ramping up your knowledge of IBM, particularly from an organizational structure standpoint, even the most complex clients will seem easy to navigate.

Game Changer #7: Seek to understand how industry leaders organize their businesses, and how specific functions either do or do not run across geographies, business units, or product lines and why.

Game Changer #8: Match industry knowledge with the specific value proposition of your company to win credibility and open opportunities with senior executives.

Game Changer #9: Visit Google's website for an incredible amount of information concerning all of their products. Google's moon-shot projects are spawning fledgling industries of their own and can be fascinating conversation starters.

Game Changer #10: See how Amazon and other industry leaders are investing their money. This can provide early insight into the next great technology you could be discussing with clients.

Game Changer #11: Take some time to investigate the acquisition history and especially recent acquisitions of industry leaders. This will give you a full picture of their go-to-market strategy and insight into what they're likely to do next.

Game Changer #12: eMarketer is a must-read if you are in the digital space. Analyst reports like Gartner and Forrester are invaluable as well, because chances are that your clients are reading them to stack rank companies during their purchase decisions. If your clients are reading an industry publication, so should you.

Game Changer #13: Technology is a major factor in sales innovation. This includes advancement in sales tools and processes, which are instantly propagated over LinkedIn, embedded within CRM systems, streamlined in mobile apps, keystroked via browser plug-ins, and enabled through shared documents. Technology continues to drive automation into outreach, calendaring, and analysis.

Game Changer #14: Demonstrate your dedication and caring for your client's success early in the process by spending time to get ingrained within their business and focusing on how to drive results.

Game Changer #15: Getting a signature on a huge contract is cause for celebration, but being an effective salesperson means a lot more than that. You have to be willing to address the less glorious details with your client's best interest at heart when things go awry.

Game Changer #16: Caring will improve your collaboration, which will in turn add meaning and fulfillment to your work.

Game Changer #17: Reviewing static product documents and specifications is not as memorable or useful without seeing how products come to life for your customers. Only then, can you truly understand the product—what it is, what it does, and what it means for your customers.

Game Changer #18: Consider caring to be the foundation of your sales success. It is the starting point that makes everything more achievable.

Game Changer #19: It's a waste of valuable time to incessantly look up who to contact or decide what call to make next. Instead, create a reliable system that drives continuous action, test it, retest, and iterate over time.

Game Changer #20: To ensure you don't get overly focused on small or large transactions, create periodic checkpoints (perhaps every month or so) to ensure you're balancing your time properly.

Game Changer #21: Track down the contract from a top deal, pour through every single detail, and visualize how you would go about arriving at the same with your prospects.

Game Changer #22: Resist the urge to ignore frameworks as inconsequential because they can add significant value to your skillset as a salesperson.

Game Changer #23: Practice makes perfect with proven frameworks.

Game Changer #24: Be flexible in your approach to meetings. Read the room for reactions to your presentation. If the client doesn't appear to be responding favorably, be prepared to shift the conversation appropriately.

Game Changer #25: A horrible meeting could be the sign of a broader issue affecting all of your sales cycles. When this happens, take some time to assess and adjust immediately.

Game Changer #26: Revisit any horrible meetings you've had in the past. Think about how you can hold yourself accountable and improve your approach to build better habits to prevent similar missteps from happening in the future.

Game Changer #27: Expect and embrace change by stepping outside of your situation to see the big picture for your company, team, and yourself. Bide your time, keep an open mind, adjust your approach, and course-correct when necessary.

Game Changer #28: Expect delivery shortfalls or missed client expectations to get blamed on sales. Dive deep into your client's expectations during the sales process, clearly document them, and conscientiously transition the deal accordingly.

Game Changer #29: While acquisitions and reorganizations can cause periods of uncertainty and disruption, they can also create opportunities to build new skills, develop new relationships, close new types of deals, and fill new roles.

Game Changer #30: You can't win every client over. Sometimes, it's better to just move on.

Game Changer #31: If you're in a positive work environment, where you're working with great people, learning a lot, and making good money, savor it!

Game Changer #32: During tough times, develop a regular practice for writing down the things for which you are grateful.

Game Changer #33: When going through a period of intense struggle—personal or professional—write down the issues and create a plan of action. Do not let it spin in your head.

Game Changer #34: No matter how well you run your sales process, you can't avoid tough conversations. Get comfortable and learn to anticipate them to lessen their potential for negative impact.

Game Changer #35: Interactions that make you feel the most uncomfortable can have the biggest impact. Run towards them.

Game Changer #36: Clients are always looking for new insights that inspire them. If you can deliver insights that align to your product, your clients will take action.

Game Changer #37: Average salespeople sell products. Great salespeople reframe and educate to challenge their client's perspective, and they do it with credibility that leads to positive change.

Game Changer #38: You'll know you've mastered initiating tough conversations when you routinely convert them into moments of deal progression, expansion, and creation.

Game Changer #39: Attack risk early and throughout the sales cycle. Become familiar with all the ways your deal can get derailed, so you can anticipate and adjust accordingly.

Game Changer #40: Put yourself in your client's shoes and make sure to understand and eliminate all the reasons why they might not be able to sign.

Game Changer #41: What you don't know about the deal can kill it. Don't let Happy Ears stop you from identifying risks early and attacking them before they derail the whole process.

Game Changer #42: Make it a habit to brainstorm with your team what the risks are and how you will overcome them.

Game Changer #43: Create a complete list of risks associated with your specific product or solution to capture the vast majority of potential deal killers.

Game Changer #44: While focusing on risk, be careful not to zero in on a specific teammate, partner, or team. Instead of casting blame and creating tension, focus on the actions that need to be taken to bring the deal home.

Game Changer #45: While brainstorming what might go wrong, never lose your optimism and excitement for how you can help your client succeed.

Game Changer #46: Assemble your deal team expansively across departments, levels of management, and external parties.

Game Changer #47: Adopt the behaviors and tactics of those you admire and make them your own. There are many paths to strong leadership, and this will help you find your path.

Game Changer #48: Carefully consider each individual's role on the team. Understand their specific strengths and weaknesses. Fill gaps where needed and position them for success.

Game Changer #49: Always keep an open mind to feedback from clients and colleagues.

Game Changer #50: Rely on your individual strengths as a team leader and find others you can trust to cover your weaknesses with their strengths.

Game Changer #51: Meeting key people in each department is a great way to establish internal relationships across the business for when you need critical help during the deal cycle. Build those interdepartmental relationships right away. Don't wait until the deal calls for it, because by then, it might be too late.

Game Changer #52: Know how and when to pull executives in without creating unnecessary risk and wasted energy. Make an ask, highlight the risks, and define the outcome.

Game Changer #53: When it comes to business partners, it's worth searching for the diamond in the rough. Look for industry expertise, a differentiated capability, or a trustworthy individual with a direct relationship to their CEO to get the job done.

Game Changer #54: Don't be single threaded in your approach. Make sure the team is exploring all options for a solution to meet the holistic needs of the client.

Game Changer #55: Occasionally, you may run into a weak link on your team or an individual that actively causes problems. Nothing good will come from calling them out or embarrassing them, but keeping them onboard could compound the disruption and damage morale. Find a way to discreetly manage them away from your dream team.

Game Changer #56: The more complex the transaction, the more energy you should expend on capturing hidden value.

Game Changer #57: Some sources of value may be common across clients, yet there are always new interpretations, prioritization, and sources for you to discover. Each deal has its own unique value fingerprint.

Game Changer #58: By focusing on abundance and expanding the pie vs. scarcity and zero-sum game, you dramatically increase your chances of capturing hidden value.

Game Changer #59: Go outside of your role and product to uncover new sources of value.

Game Changer #60: Don't hesitate to step outside your role to fill any gaps you uncover that may benefit your client or your entire client base.

Game Changer #61: Mega Deals will "die" several times along the way. Don't panic. Regroup with your team, form a plan, and re-engage with your client.

Game Changer #62: Thinking big about your offer requires thinking big about all the variables involved.

Game Changer #63: It's imperative to be as thorough as possible to make sure your offer is sound, because there will be surprises anytime you push the established boundaries.

APPENDIX B

RECOMMENDED RESOURCES

The Four by Scott Galloway

The Singularity Is Near by Ray Kurzweil

Bold by Peter Diamandis

Good to Great by Jim Collins

The Minto Pyramid Principle by Barbara Minto

Secrets of Question Based Selling by Thomas Freese

The Challenger Sale by Matthew Dixon and Brent Adamson

Getting More by Stuart Diamond

DISCLAIMER

The views expressed in this book are solely those of the author. All copyrights, trademarks, brands, names, symbols, logos, and designs depicted in this book are the property of their respective owners. They are used for identification and reference purposes only and do not imply endorsement or approval of this book.

ABOUT THE AUTHOR

DAVID PERRY advises world-class brands on how to transform their marketing organizations through the acquisition and effective use of enterprise technology solutions. Since 1999, David has worked with more than one hundred companies across a wide range of industries including financial services, consumer products, technology, and healthcare. In the process, he's driven over $125 million in new business and managed revenues.

In addition to his work in sales, David also serves as a startup advisor and investor and organizes technology entrepreneurship events in New York City. David received his MBA from the Johnson Graduate School of Management at Cornell University and lives in New York City with his wife, Arianne, and their son, James.

To access additional *Game of Sales* materials, visit https://www.gameofsalesbook.com.

Made in the USA
Middletown, DE
11 August 2021